A Round In My Mind

The Golfer and The Sport Psychologist
on The Jubilee Course at St. Andrews

Mark Wilson

Paul McCarthy

Oakamoor
Publishing

Published in 2015 by Oakamoor Publishing, an imprint of Bennion Kearny Limited.

Copyright © Oakamoor Publishing 2015

ISBN: 978-1-910773-10-9

Published by Oakamoor Publishing, an imprint of Bennion Kearny Limited
6 Woodside
Churnet View Road
Oakamoor
ST10 3AE

www.BennionKearny.com

Without 'doing a Barry McGuigan', I'd like to thank Dad for instilling in me a love of sport; Mum for harnessing my passion for learning and writing; Nic for sharing this journey with me; and Liv and Ani for inspiring me to do better.

Mark

To Lesley, Liam, Euan, and Niamh for all time

Paul

About the Authors

Dr Mark Wilson is Associate Professor of Experimental Psychology & Human Movement Science at the University of Exeter with a particular interested in how people learn visually-guided skills and how these skills might break down under pressure.

Dr Paul McCarthy is the first-ever resident Sport Psychologist at the home of golf - St Andrews Links - and a Lecturer in Psychology at Glasgow Caledonian University. He consults with golfers at all levels – amateur and professional – especially those playing on the European Tour, Challenge Tour and Ladies European Tour.

Acknowledgements

We are most grateful to Bennion Kearny for the opportunity to publish with them. And we would not be writing these acknowledgements without the guidance, support and trust in our work by James Lumsden-Cook. James has guided, and continues to guide, us around the traps into which we would normally fall. We are also indebted to Steve North, the Director of Instruction at St Andrews Links Golf Academy, for his support of our book and sport psychology within the Academy. Steve not only supports our work on the psychology of golf at St Andrews Links Golf Academy but also encourages us to find new and exciting ways to bring the psychology of golf to golfers at all levels. We are also thankful to other staff members at St Andrews Links Trust especially Laurie Watson, Communications Manager, and Lewis Willing, Digital Marketing Executive, for sourcing the hole-guide images for each chapter of this book. I (Paul) am always learning from my experiences at St Andrews Links Golf Academy through my conversations with all the support staff, golf coaches: Fintan, Kevin, Blair, David, and Scott; club fitting specialists: Adam, Greg and especially Martin Jones for the erudite conversations and soothing cups of coffee!

Table of Contents

Foreword

Improving your golf game requires a fine balance between the services that are available and the services that are right for each golfer. These services might include a swing coach, putting coach, strength and conditioning coach, physiotherapist, sport psychologist and dietician. Each service is a spoke in the wheel of excellence and if one spoke is missing, the wheel loses its strength and stability. It remains the golfer's choice to judge which of these services best address their needs within the game. Here at St Andrews Links Golf Academy, we are committed to offer golfers the services that bring their games to next level.

One spoke in the wheel of excellence that is often missing is the psychological support provided by a charted sport psychologist. Unfortunately, some golfers are still unsure about how a sport psychologist works and the benefits a sport psychologist can offer their games. In this unique book on the psychology of golf, Dr Paul McCarthy and Dr Mark Wilson bring us face to face with the work that a sport psychologist might do with a golfer out on the golf course. This fictional account of an amateur golfer working with a sport psychologist on the golf course mimics the real life experiences of the support available to any golfer at any level. If the best golfers in the world benefit from working with sport psychologists, it seems sensible to learn from their best practice and move your game to the next level. After all, who doesn't want to lower their scores and enjoy their time on the golf course?

Steve North. Director of Instruction, St Andrews Links Golf Academy

Prologue – The Car Park

This is a story about Chris Marriott, a 4-handicap golfer who plays a round of golf at his local links – the Jubilee Course at St Andrews – with a sport psychologist, Dr James MacAndrew. James works with golfers – from the European Tour to satellite tours in the UK and Europe, and amateur golfers of all levels. During this round of golf, Chris and James share their experiences as the round of golf unfolds.

James arranged to meet Chris at the driving range forty-five minutes before his tee time, but he arrived just fifteen minutes before. Chris darted from the driver's seat to the boot of his car, ripping at his bag of clubs that was tangled with his son's scooter. Eventually, the bag emerged, along with a bucket and spade from a trip to the beach the previous day. Chris fumbled through the large pocket on his bag where he had left his shoes from his last round of golf three days before. It had rained that evening and the freshly cut grass was still clinging to the cleats of his golf shoes. He smashed the soles of the shoes together three or four times before sitting down on the edge of the boot to put them on. James could see Chris was flustered, so he walked slowly to his car, allowing Chris some time to compose himself and get himself ready for the round of golf. They shook hands, and as they did so, Chris began his apology:

'So sorry, James; I thought I had more time to prepare this morning, but my wife popped out to the shops and was back late – so I was minding the two monsters! It's not how I usually get ready.' James replied calmly, 'Life doesn't stop because we have a round of golf to play.' James prompted Chris to take a moment to prepare.

Chris enquired, 'What shall we do now?' To which James replied, 'What would you normally do now?'

'I would probably just hit some putts so I am close to the first tee because I don't want to miss my tee time.'

'OK, let's begin there.'

James wanted to see how Chris usually prepared for a round of golf. He wondered whether this rushed preparation was more usual than Chris admitted. It is often the case that golfers disproportionately display their best side to the sport psychologist – the 'perfect' side, as it were – rather than who they really are. A lifetime being the person your parents want you to be; what your teachers wanted you to be; what your boss wants you to be. It can be exhausting.

Ripples of these thoughts were entering Chris' mind. Chris felt a little uneasy. As he rolled one or two putts on the green, he thought, 'Oh, my routine! Oh hell! I should be doing my routine. It's the first thing I read in his (Dr MacAndrew's) book: *With Golf in Mind*. I bet he can't wait to see the end of this round. He's used to watching Albert Ross sinking putt after putt on the practice ground of the Old Course as he prepares for the Dunhill Links or the Scottish Open at Royal Aberdeen. And now he has to endure my appalling putting stroke. Damn it – why did I contact him in the first place!'

James enquired, 'How are you feeling?' Without hesitation, Chris replied, 'Oh fine.' It was a response Chris unthinkingly offered to people he met. He'd always been fine. When he was asked to do extra hours at work, 'Oh, that's fine'; when his wife wanted him to look after the children while she went shopping with friends, and he couldn't watch the football, it was 'fine'. When his father demanded he assist within the family business during the summer holidays, and he couldn't go to the beach with his friends – it was always fine.

James queried a second time with sincerity: 'How are you feeling?' Chris felt that his response ought to be sincere too.

'To tell you the truth, James, I'm not feeling so good. I….I….I have played golf for the past thirty years, you know, ever since I was a kid. And I love golf, but it just hurts me now. I'm not as good as I thought I would be; I'm just not good enough.'

James replied, 'Not good enough?' in an enquiring tone, reflecting the point for Chris.

'Yeah, just not good enough to play what I think I can play. I'm not succeeding; it's embarrassing. You'd be embarrassed to play golf and show your scorecard to the lads. You'd be ashamed of your scores in the clubhouse because you used to be good.'

James recognised the distance Chris placed between what was happening and to whom it was happening. Chris created this distance with 'You'd be embarrassed...You'd be ashamed....'. James tried to capture what Chris was saying: 'Golf, it would seem, is hurting you now; you're feeling that you are not worthy to play golf when your scores are not as good as you would like them to be and what others might expect from you, because you were good before?'

Chris nodded as he walked to pick up his ball. 'It's funny.' Chris laughed as he flicked the ball into the air from the ground using the back of his putter and dropped it into his trouser pocket. 'You're right, you know. You've just captured what I have been feeling for quite a while now. How could anyone play golf well thinking and feeling as I do? I guess that's why you work with the pros.'

James enjoyed the compliment and smiled, slightly embarrassed, and paused for a while.

'That's kind of you to say so; I guess I've learned about myself too – talking honestly with my clients. They have helped me to see myself – the good and the bad.' With that, they both laughed heartily as they walked to the first tee.

Hole 1:
Willie Auchterlonie (367-yard par 4)

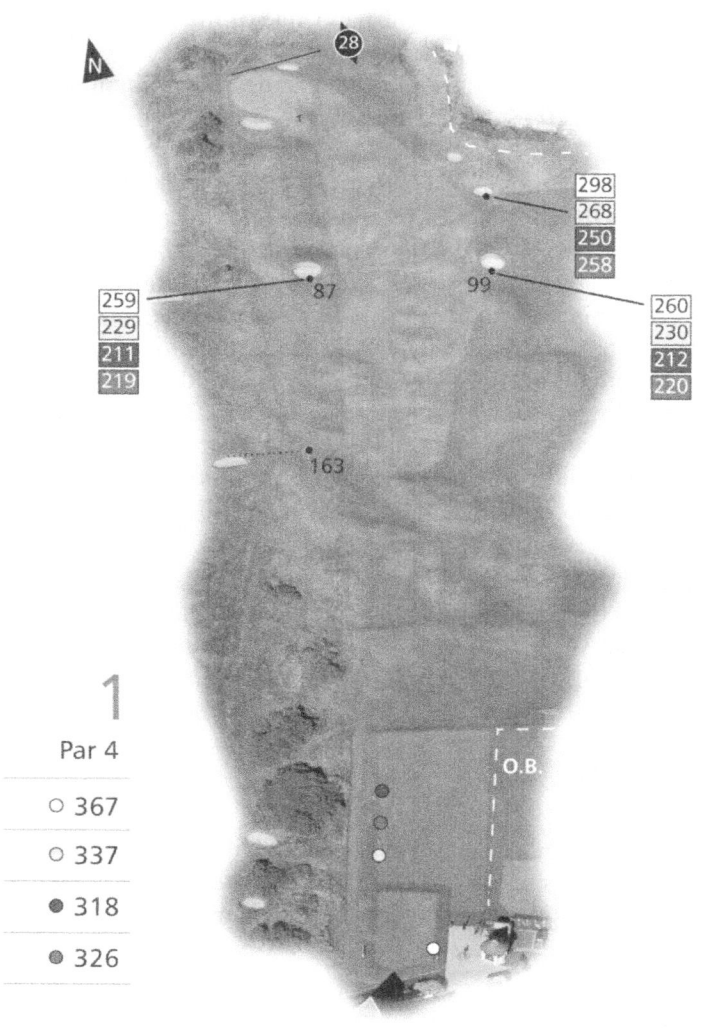

The first tee was clear now, a two-ball had just left, and both players were in the middle of the fairway preparing for their second shots. Chris teed up his ball to play the 367-yard par 4 with a slight dogleg left to a raised green. With a good drive, Chris would be within pitching wedge distance (about 120 yards) and a gilt-edged chance of a birdie – but it had to be a good drive. There was silence between Chris and James because James didn't want to interfere as Chris prepared to play the tee shot as he would have extemporaneously. Chris' natural shot was a draw so he used to tee his ball on the right-hand side of the tee and let the ball fly out to the right before it curved back towards the centre of the fairway – even a little towards the left-hand side – allowing him to regard the green directly for his approach shot.

Chris took two practice swings. He did so because he had seen one of his favourite Tour professionals – Ernie Els – do so at the recent Scottish Open. He set himself up to the ball, glanced down the fairway and then back to the ball. Then he repeated the glance down the fairway, and when he brought his eyes back to the ball, he moved the clubhead away and unleashed a cracking drive. The ball soared to the right-hand side of the fairway, turning gracefully and swooping with a delicate bounce forward on the downslope of a ridge on the fairway, stopping ninety yards from the green. Chris plucked his tee from the ground and said, 'You're working your magic already – it's been quite a while since I drove off the first tee as well as I did there. It's birdie time now!'

James noticed the elation in Chris. He noticed how his shoulders were pushed back and his chest puffed out. The fourball waiting at the first tee congratulated him with 'Golf shot!' and another shouted 'That's Bubba long!' He slipped his bag onto his shoulders and waited for James to speak.

'Chris, those boys enjoyed it!'

'I guess so. It's nice to hear that – it's been a while, you know. And that's one of the things about golf – golfers applaud good shots even when they are competing against you. In how many sports does that happen?'

'You enjoy good shots?' James enquired tentatively.

'Who doesn't?'

'Yes, a fair point. I suppose what I am asking is that a good shot is satisfying to you and there's an extra buzz if other golfers see it too?'

Guessing that James was hinting at something about what it means to have others recognise how well you play golf, Chris explained: 'Well, I used to just like hitting good shots. There is something so satisfying in the feeling of getting through the ball and watching it soar with a lovely draw through the air – like a drug it is. I'd hit for hours down at the range, never really bothering who was about. I was lost in my own world. I was Tom Watson, I was Freddie Couples, and I was Tom Kite. Other golfers would enthuse, "You've got a lovely swing – silky smooth." Sometimes, I could overhear some of the older golfers at the club saying, "Take a look at his swing – pure class – even at his age. I tell you, if he doesn't make it, nobody will." and "He works so hard, he's like Faldo." And for someone who didn't get much praise at home, I was hooked on the stuff at the golf club. I'd do anything to get more of it – anything.'

James pondered on what might be unfolding now for Chris – emotionally, at least. A flashback to his teenage years when the game seemed so enjoyable, lost in his own world playing golf. His golf performances brought adulation from those around him, and the future seemed laden with riches – golfing riches. James felt that the rich past and the poor present might not be helping Chris to cope with golf now, with the disappointment and regret of what might have been. This last point was particularly heartbreaking because when Chris was growing up he played golf successfully at each age group and lost in the semi-final of the under-18 national championship – a highlight of his golf career. He was somebody – he was good at golf. And the boy he beat in the quarter-finals of that national championship 4&3, and twice before in similar events, was now a stalwart on the European Tour. Chris used to feel sorry for him because he beat him three years in a row in national championship match-play. The boy tried so hard but didn't have the faculties to defeat Chris.

'And now?' James enquired.

'Well, now, all I've got are the memories. Oh, and this putter – I haven't changed it, but it used to work better then.'

Chris and James were now standing a few feet from his ball and Chris said, 'Will I just play as I normally do?'

'Yes, as you normally do.'

Chris appeared constrained in his practice swings. Ninety yards was more than a full gap wedge for him so he had chosen his pitching wedge and was trying to make a shorter, smoother swing. He stepped into the ball, glanced at the target and back at his ball about eight times, and then struck the ball. It set off steeply – heading towards the flag, drawing more and more as it reached the green, eventually missing the green short left and rolling into the deep bunker there. It left James with a challenging up and down to save par.

Before James said a word, Chris defensively uttered, 'From the sublime to the ridiculous – nothing new there,' James paused for a moment as Chris examined his clubface, before reflecting: 'Is this pattern usual for your golf shots?'

'It is now. I knew the shot I needed, but I couldn't commit to it; and I was so eager to see the ball hit the green, I was up and out of my shot before it left the clubface – so silly, so annoying. This was a birdie hole.'

'And now...'

'Now I'll be lucky to walk off with a six from there. I know it is the worst side to be on this hole and, lo and behold, I'm there!'

James didn't want to interfere at this stage of the round and consultation. He resisted offering unsolicited advice and pontificating about the psychology of excellence in golf. James wished for Chris to relate his story – as a golfer and as a person. He needed Chris to reflect on how he regarded himself on the golf course and all those ways of thinking that marred his game. Destructive thinking that is illogical and irrational pervades golf. James had heard this destructive thinking from Chris and many other golfers. It ranged from rigid demands (e.g., I must get a birdie on this hole), to awfulising (e.g., A bogey is awful) and low frustration tolerance (e.g., I can't stand it when my shot does not go where I want it to).

Chris trudged to his ball with his sand wedge dragging along the ground. He had the air of a man who had lost all hope. In the bunker, Chris peered up from where he stood and could just see the top portion of the flag on the far side of the green, and said, 'Here goes nothing!' With that final proclamation, he swung his club and the ball shot into the air, landing softly, just inches from the hole. Chris couldn't see the ball but felt it was good and raced up the bank to catch a glimpse of it landing. It had landed before he arrived, and he looked astonished at what he had just achieved. 'Now that is one lucky shot,' he laughed. He didn't even need his putter to tap the ball into the hole – par 4, done and dusted.

As they walked to the next tee, James reflected on what he had just seen.

'You had a shot to the green that slipped off the edge and left you with a tricky up and down. You felt that a double bogey would be the best you could score from there. Yet, I've just watched you write the number four on your scorecard.'

Left with the echo of this statement, Chris explained himself, 'I guess I didn't realise that I was capable of getting up and down; or more accurately, I was wallowing in self-pity for a poor approach shot and letting myself off the hook, rather than focusing on what I had to do – fighting for everything. OK, lesson learned!'

Hole 2:
Whinny Knowe (360-yard par 4)

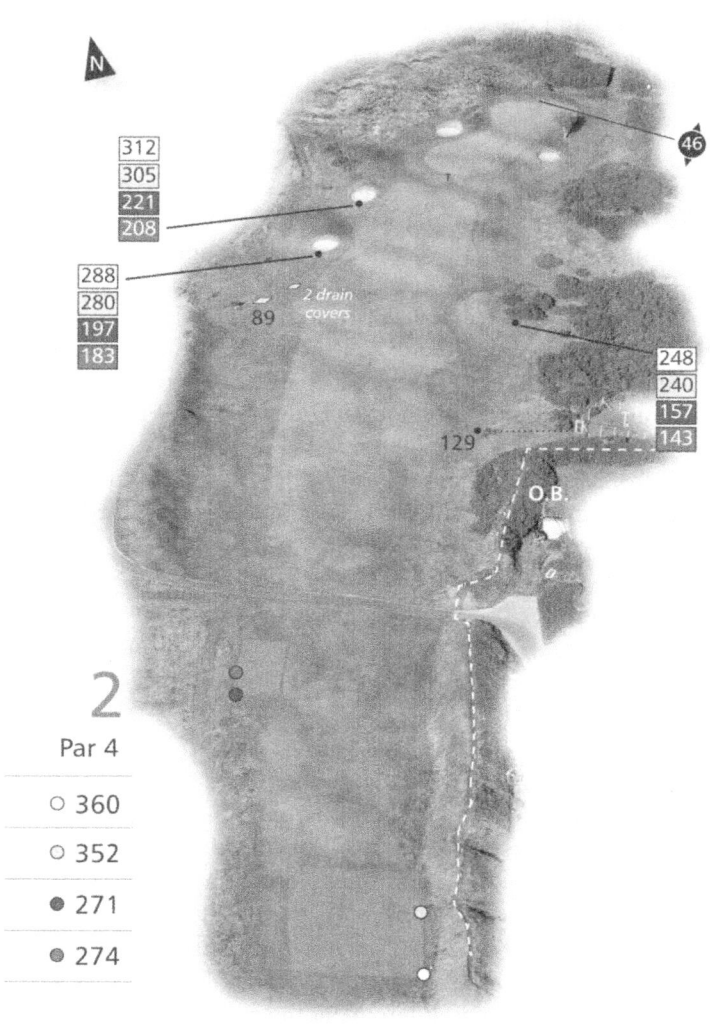

312
305
221
208

288
280
197
183

2 drain
covers

89

248
240
157
143

129

O.B.

2

Par 4

○ 360

○ 352

● 271

● 274

46

The second hole was another short par 4. A solid drive would leave Chris with a wedge into the centre of the green, which was guarded with bunkers at the front and thick rough at the back. This green was two-tiered, with the high portion sloping gently to a sharp incline leading to the lower portion of the green. The two-ball ahead were in the fairway, so James and Chris discussed the challenge of the hole ahead.

Chris began, 'It doesn't look like much, does it? But this hole has caught out more players than I can count. You see, it's a wedge or 9-iron approach shot most of the time, depending on the wind, and the danger is mostly at the front. I know what I need to do here – club up on my approach shot.'

After another solid drive – slightly held up by a light breeze – Chris was left with 110 yards to the pin and 130 yards to the back edge of the green. Chris and James were now standing close to the ball as Chris began to select a club. James noticed a slight hesitancy in Chris' club selection. Chris lifted his gap wedge, dropped it back into his bag and picked up his pitching wedge, then flicked back to this gap wedge. Chris mentioned that he was playing to the 'fat' part of the green on the top tier to avoid the bunkers. The pin was located on the lower tier near the front right bunker. Chris hit his shot high, and as it continued to climb, it lost distance and dropped sharply in the face of the front right bunker. 'Argh...damn that gust of wind,' Chris lamented as he walked back to his bag.

James didn't feel a gust of wind; in fact, it was quite calm with a constant, light breeze. In any case, he was concerned about Chris' explanation. He enquired, 'The ball dropped quite sharply on your wedge shot; is that typical for you?'

Chris thought about it for a few seconds, 'I suppose it does, but I've probably not thought about how it drops. Feeling that gust of wind, I should have clubbed up as I said back on the tee.' James felt that Chris had made a sensible decision '...to use enough club' as they discussed the shot beforehand, yet he had chosen his gap wedge, rather than his pitching wedge, when he arrived at his ball in the fairway.

'Chris, it sounds as though you knew what the right course of action was at the beginning but changed your mind when you pulled out your gap wedge. I wonder what you were thinking about at that moment.'

'I thought it was the right decision, alright,' Chris snapped.

'I gather you might be annoyed by your decision and regret the outcome or, perhaps, you are annoyed by what I said?'

'No, I'm not annoyed about what you said at all.'

'But I sense you have something more to say?'

'Okay, you got me. You see, I was feeling confident after getting up and down on the last hole, and my ego saw a birdie opportunity. With the pin at the front, I thought it would be a full gap wedge, hit perfectly. I thought it would be at the foot of the flag. I don't think I hit it as well as I could have and it came up short. I should have used my pitching wedge, and now I'm trying not to think about the bunker shot and what will happen, but I fear a dropped shot here.'

'Do you feel your emotions played the shot before you had a chance to choose the best option for you right now?'

'I guess so; I am playing the shot as the golfer I wish I was, rather than the golfer I am right now. I suppose it's just something I have to come to terms with.'

James felt Chris was disappointed about this realisation. 'You seem quite unhappy with that realisation.'

'I am sad – I'm playing someone else's game rather than my own. I'm playing to look good to anyone who cares to watch. I'm making bad decisions and what I get is bad golf from a bad golfer.'

James was aware that Chris might be drawing a harsh conclusion (or exaggerating) to explain the event that had just happened. If Chris had hit the gap wedge perfectly, his ball might well have been at the foot of the flag and this conversation might not be happening – had that outcome prevailed. Sometimes, the vagaries of golf feed the tale of woe for the golfer; sometimes, it's best to avoid the microanalysis of every shot so that we can account for the imperfections humans experience when playing sports. On this occasion, Chris can choose to blame himself for the outcome or he can choose to learn from the experience – especially, how his biased thinking creates unhelpful emotions and actions. This one shot does not make Chris a bad golfer, and neither does one shot make Chris a good golfer. James wanted to help Chris to avoid labelling himself as 'bad' and felt this might be something to discuss as the round progressed.

Chris and James were now standing in the bunker assessing the shot. Chris began by saying, 'My ego wants to pop this up high and drop it softly by the hole.'

'Only *by* the hole?' as if to say he thought Chris' ego would want to drop it into the hole for a birdie. Chris laughed, 'Now that's an ego.'

James enquired about Chris' choice and asked, 'What would you choose to do if you were playing golf confidently?' This question is known as a contrast; it quickly helps the golfer to understand what he would think, feel and do if he were feeling confident. Chris smiled and said, 'It's funny that you ask that question because if I were feeling confident, I would probably look at the lie of the ball and make a sensible assessment to get the ball up and down.'

'Shall we go with that decision, Chris?'

'It sounds good to me.'

Chris retraced his steps to his bag, picked up his sand wedge and stood by the greenside bunker, rehearsing practice swings. James identified the 'confident, young golfer' emerging in Chris as he descended into the bunker. With multiple glances at the flag and the landing spot, Chris smoothly splashed the ball out of the sand, landing it softly – seven feet from the pin. Chris smiled as he knocked the sand from his cleats and placed the club back into his bag.

Chris eased the head cover off his putter and walked over to mark his ball. He placed the line on his ball on his intended line and stepped back from the ball to make two practice strokes. James didn't want to interfere at this stage of the putting routine, so he let Chris prepare and execute the shot. Chris stepped into the ball and made one last practice stroke. Then he glanced at the hole one last time and stroked the ball. It didn't deviate from its line and dropped in the front door.

'Two pars already – I like where this is going!' Chris exclaimed.

While the pair ambled to the next tee, Chris mentioned to James that he estimated he was 'playing more aggressive golf, fighting for his place in the game' and asked whether James agreed. 'Does that sound right to you, James?'

'I guess the question I have for you, Chris, is whether it sounds right to you.'

'Yes, I suppose it does. I am starting to find my golfing-self out here.'

Hole 3:
The Skelp (546-yard par 5)

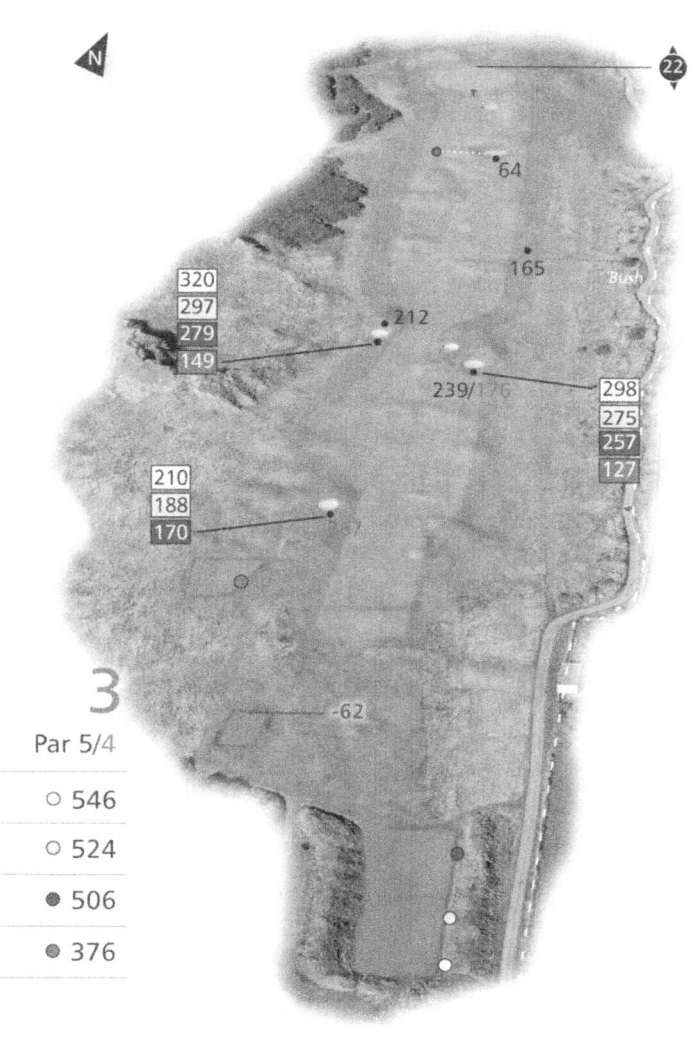

Par 5/4

○ 546

○ 524

● 506

● 376

The third hole was a long par 5 and it was important to get a good drive away. Chris was clearly thinking along these lines as he drew his driver out of the bag on the tee box.

'Right, here we go. Nice draw, just like the first two, but give it a wee bit extra.'

Again, James felt it was best to let things unfold naturally, rather than interrupt Chris as he went through his pre-shot preparation. It was important for James to get a sense of how Chris reacted to 'success and failure' and how it affected the way he played. So far things had worked out well for Chris, even when he had experienced sticky moments. It is easy to have positive thoughts and feel confident when things are working out; however, things become more of a challenge when results don't match expectations.

Chris went through the same 'Ernie Els' pre-shot routine as he had done previously and stepped up to the ball with a brisk, purposeful stride. Two further glances down the fairway and then a fast swing at the ball.

'Oh no! I came over that...get out! Don't go in there! *Oh for fuck's sake!*'

Unfortunately, and as many golfers can attest to, the ball failed to listen to his instructions and plunged, after one bounce, into the closest fairway bunker, just over 200 yards out.

'Sorry about the language, James; I just hate it when I do that. I mean... I know a long drive is important on this hole and here I go duck-hooking it into the nearest bunker. Idiot!'

'Don't worry about the language – I am Irish after all. It is part of my culture.'

'Ha ha. OK, thanks...but I mean... it's just so frustrating. I sort of knew that drive was going to be bad. I just had a feeling; you know...my swing just felt fast and out of control right from the start. When that happens, my bad shot is the duck-hook, as perfectly demonstrated there. I should have just stopped and re-started.'

Chris forcefully returned his driver into his bag and angrily slung it onto his back; '…especially, as you had already warned me about my decision making on the last hole. Talk about not learning from my mistakes, eh?'

'Well, there is no doubt that that wasn't the best contact you made so far today, Chris. I'm interested in what you think happened. Let's start with this negative feeling you mentioned just before your swing.'

'Doesn't everyone get them? You know, when you just feel that the swing is not right and you still go ahead with it like an idiot…even though you have this…this…sort of premonition.'

As he walked along the fairway, James took a moment to reply, sensing that Chris was again trying to distance himself from his negative thoughts through his language; referring to 'you' instead of 'I'.

'Well, I am not sure anyone can see the future, but I agree that it is interesting how what we think, and how we feel, can influence our behaviours so powerfully. In fact, I guess that a lot of what I try to do is help people explore these moments and be aware of their influence on how they feel and how they play. So, while it is still fresh in your mind, could you tell me a little more about why you seem so annoyed with that drive?'

'Well…I guess I hate the fact that golf is hard enough for me right now without me making it worse. I didn't do what I should have done. I just went ahead and followed my routine, even though I felt sort of stiff and mechanical right from the start. Even my practice swings didn't feel great but I thought I should get on with it, anyway. Then I was really aware of how stiff things felt in my backswing and, even though this was like a red flag, I just went through with the shot anyway. Straight into this demon of a pot bunker… Oh, and perfect – I'm right up against the face. Typical!'

James was aware that Chris was again focusing on the outcome of his shot and things that were uncontrollable (the ball being in a bad spot), rather than the lessons that could be learned from what happened before the shot – when he still had control over how the shot was played. He really wanted to further explore Chris' thought processes about the drive, as he felt there were some interesting issues related to Chris' expectations of himself; his relationship with golf, in general; and specific issues about his preparation and his routine, raised by what he had said. However, Chris had already clambered down into the deep bunker and was preparing to splash out sideways. James made a mental note of Chris' response and stopped himself from making too many assumptions about what these comments might mean. If he listened carefully enough, Chris would reveal more about his underlying concerns as the round unfolded.

Chris splashed the ball back out on the fairway, and made straight for his bag to select a club for his long third shot. 'Well, there goes a wasted shot. I'll just knock it up there now with my lucky hybrid...OK, let's do your stuff.' Golfers often have 'lucky' clubs, or at least 'hot' clubs, where they feel more confident of a successful outcome. However, it is often interesting to note the effect that these beliefs have on the way they approach the shot; with more confidence, more relaxation, less negative thoughts whirring around...no wonder the swing is better and the outcome more positive. Clearly, this also happens in the other direction, where negative expectations about a club or a shot lead to a self-affirming bias...a poor swing and a poor outcome. The awareness of such effects can be a powerful lesson in improving consistency of thought control and performance.

While Chris may not have been aware of the ensuing changes in his posture, his swing, or his grip, which led to a great contact with the ball, the 'lucky hybrid' lived up to its name. Chris hit a beautifully struck draw that put him in the perfect spot to attack the pin with his wedge from 110 yards. His confidence clearly still high from the previous shot, Chris wasted no time with his fourth, almost hitting the hole, and running just four feet past the flag. Extravagantly kissing the face of the club, Chris beamed over to James, 'That's more like it!' As he approached the green, he finally saw just how close he had ended up to the hole... He eagerly removed the head cover from his putter and strode purposively over to mark his ball. 'It looks like I might just scramble another par after all. Scrappy, but they all count.'

Again, James was carefully observing the rollercoaster of emotions that Chris appeared to experience on the course. While it is, of course, natural to feel better about good – as opposed to bad – shots, better-developed emotional control can help to flatten out these spikes, producing the environment for greater consistency. In effect, developing better awareness of emotional triggers can protect against the vicious circle of poor emotional control leading to inconsistent performance leading to bigger emotional swings and greater inconsistency... etc. etc. Not only is this vicious circle hard on a golf score, but also, it is even harder on the human being involved, who puts him/herself through the emotional wringer. When feelings of self-worth are also determined by the inconsistent nature of where this small white ball ends up, it is not surprising that golf can be a frustrating endeavour when 'outcome is king'.

As James went to remove the flag, he felt that it might be appropriate to start to prompt Chris towards thinking less about the outcome and more about the processes he could control. 'You made a great swing there, Chris. It looked like everything was relaxed and in control, and you knew exactly what you wanted to do. How did it feel to you?'

'Yeah, that was sweet... just what I was trying to do. I just tried to swing easy and ... there you go.' Chris slipped off the putter head cover and extracted his pitchfork from his pocket (the first time in the round). He took pride in fixing the pitch mark correctly. It was, after all, just a few inches from the hole directly behind the flag.

Chris had started lining up his putt, so James decided to pause and continue the conversation on the walk to the next tee. After two practice putts, Chris addressed the ball and made a tentative, stab of a putt, missing on the low side of the hole by more than a couple of inches. 'No! Stay down on it, for God's sake!' He tapped it in and angrily thrust his hand into the cup to remove the ball before throwing it hard into the banking at the side of green. 'This is what it is like, James...from hero to zero in seconds...no wonder I can't return a decent card.'

James paused and waited for Chris to retrieve his ball before replying. 'It certainly was an *exciting* hole to watch, even if it was tough for you to play. I wonder if you would mind going through it again with me, while we walk to the tee.'

'What would you like to know?' asked Chris, hesitantly.

James took a moment to consider. It is often not easy to know where to start when reviewing a particular incident with clients. There is always the concern that something might be missed or that you, as a sport psychologist, will lead them away from what might be the most important issues. 'Well, what stands out for you, given that you have carded a six there on the stroke three hole?'

'I guess a six is a decent return on the third…especially after that bloody drive! You need to drive well round here or you'll never score.'

James felt that this moment was appropriate to start challenging some of Chris' perceptions of his golf game. Perceptions are not 'facts' and can be tested if they create an environment for 'stinking thinking'; where bad decisions and emotionally driven behaviours are the likely outcomes.

'Yes, that wasn't your best drive, but what happened next?'

'Well, I chipped out … hit a nice hybrid and then a 9-iron to four feet I guess.'

'So, you could still have made par despite "that bloody drive"?' James asked, with a small smile on his lips.

'If I hadn't mucked up the putt, you mean?' replied Chris sardonically. 'I guess I see what you are trying to say. The hole wasn't over after the drive and I guess I need to keep reminding myself about that. I am just one good shot from getting back in it. It's hard though, as you get so wound up … For example, you won't believe this, but I am still thinking of that bloody putt now, as I am talking to you!'

'Why is that a problem for you?' James asked.

'Well, I just find it so hard being so inconsistent all the time. Look at this hole…crap drive; decent option to splash out instead of trying to take off too much from the bunker; brilliant hybrid; brilliant 9-iron; and crap putt; bogey on the card. It's exhausting playing golf in this way.'

'I would imagine it is,' replied James warmly. 'How do you think you could have made that hole less exhausting?'

'Well, apart from taking three shots onto the green and a regulation two putt, do you mean? I'm not sure, really; I was just all over the place.'

'The interesting thing, from my perspective, is that it wasn't just the ball that "was all over the place", Chris.' James allowed Chris some time to think about this comment, believing that it was important for Chris' self-awareness development that he practiced objectively assessing his own emotional responses to his golf.

'I know I get a bit uptight with bad shots but surely that is normal, isn't it, James?'

James recognised Chris' need to feel normal – whatever that might be – a typical response from players of all abilities when dealing with self-imposed limitations on their ability to succeed. It is an important step towards improved self-awareness to realise that our reactions to perceived success and failure are natural – especially given the societal influences we face. However, just because something might be natural, does not mean that is productive…

'It certainly is normal to have an automatic reaction to *good* and *bad* shots, Chris, but you have to ask yourself if it is helping you, or hurting you when it comes to how you play golf. If it is something that is non-productive, then perhaps it is something that you should explore. You mentioned that it is "exhausting" playing a hole like this last one, so on the next hole do you think you could explore your reactions to each shot just after you have played it? That might give you some clues about how you might conserve emotional energy so you don't get too mentally exhausted. OK?'

'Sure, I guess I could do that.'

Hole 4:
Crossgate (371-yard par 4)

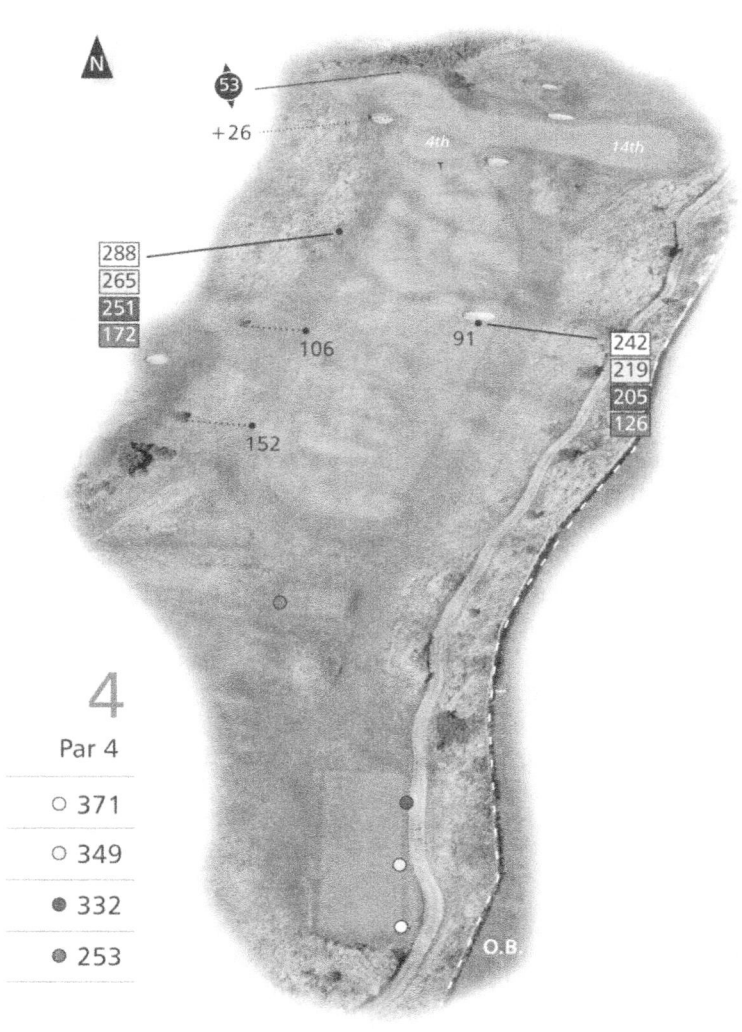

The fourth hole was easier than the third – at least on paper. But after another hooked tee shot into the left rough it was punishing for Chris – the left bunker made the approach shot to the green much more difficult from that side, with the pin in the back left portion.

'You really don't want to know what I am thinking right now, James, trust me.'

'OK, but it is interesting that just because you made the deal to discuss your reaction to shots with me, you managed to maintain your control better there – even if it was difficult for you. Rather than the outburst on the last hole, you used some humour to deflate the situation a little this time. It is really important that you recognise these small wins that you work hard for. These are the stepping stones towards better emotional control.'

'It doesn't feel like a win at the moment, but I see what you are saying. I was a bit embarrassed by my outburst on the last, so I repressed it this time. I understand what you are trying to do, but it is hard fighting against my usual reactions. I get it that the upcoming shot is the same whether I approach it in a good frame of mind or with my head still reeling from a bad shot. I get it that it is better to be settled and focused over the ball rather than re-living the last shot … it's just difficult.'

'I think you are prospering, Chris,' replied James warmly. 'It's challenging to break habits, but you are progressing and that is what is important. Lots of people do not even make this first step into action. They hope that things will change and somehow – as if by magic – their mental game will reform. Instead, they simply end up playing well or poorly, depending on how they happen to feel at a given moment – there is no consistency in the process. You did really well there. You chose how you reacted to the shot and used humour to cope with it. The next step is to think about how you would *like* to feel as you approach this next shot.'

'It is nice of you to say those kind things, James, and I must admit that I do feel a bit more positive, knowing that I can choose how to react to a shocker like that. I have always liked using humour, so it is great to know that I can use it to keep me a bit more balanced. As for this next shot, I'm already feeling pretty relaxed about it – I can only really play short right here with my 9-iron and that is something that I can handle. The green is too hard to go for from this lie with that bunker.'

Chris lived up to his prediction and put his approach shot just short of the putting surface, leaving him with a straightforward pitch and run up the length of the green. 'First job done…now to execute this pitch.' Chris made a good contact, sending the ball on line up the slope, but as it was a bit fast it rolled just past the right edge of the hole and ended up leaving another four feet putt for par.

'I guess I was a bit aggressive there but I am happy with how I have played this hole after my drive. I didn't miss by much and remembered to watch the roll of the ball after the hole to see how it moved. I am pretty confident about this putt.' Chris stepped up and holed the left to right breaking putt confidently.

'How was that for you then, Chris?' asked James, as he threw Chris back his ball from the hole.

'Well, my initial reaction is that I did pretty well – after the drive. I guess that hole was similar to the last in terms of the strategy I used after a bad drive, but it felt very different to me. I tried to remain more neutral with each shot and not get too "up" or "down". I have to say that it felt a little easier emotionally. I'm not sure exactly how I want to feel over the ball for each shot yet, but I think that I did a good job of how I reacted to the shots I played, and stayed focused enough to not let it impact on the next shot. I will definitely try to keep working on this.'

'That is really great work, Chris; remember that this is a strategy that you can keep working on for the rest of your golfing career. Sometimes, it will be easier than others, and you won't always get it perfect. Just remember that you can *choose* how you react to a shot – it doesn't have to be automatic.'

'Thank you, James. Now, if only I can get my driving sorted out … it tends to be inconsistent until I get warmed up.'

As they walked towards the tee, James took the opportunity that Chris had provided, to mention the rushed preparation to the round.

'The question I am interested in exploring is that if you think that a lack of warm-up affects your driving, Chris, what could you do about that?'

'I know I should get to the tee earlier and hit balls for an hour or whatever, just like the professionals, but I just can't find that much time. I would love to, but...life just gets in the way, James, you know. I thought I had got away with my lack of warm-up, to be honest, after that drive on the first – sometimes I am not so lucky. Today, it took a bit longer to catch up with me,'

'You make a good point, Chris, about priorities and the difficulties of managing our lives; however, what if you had got here just ten minutes earlier. Would that have helped you be more warmed-up?'

'I think I see what you are trying to say, James. I can get a fair bit of benefit from just being a wee bit more organised, without being perfect. All right ... I am going to make a promise to myself that I'll give myself at least ten minutes to warm-up before tee-time. No excuses – I can find ten minutes.'

Much of the mental game of golf involves removing self-imposed limitations, and some of these limitations are 'low hanging fruit'. Better preparation grants a more consistent platform for consistent performance. As the saying goes, 'Fail to prepare...prepare to fail'. Being more mentally and physically prepared to start the round should be the bare minimum.

Hole 5:
Hackie's Barra (162-yard par 3)

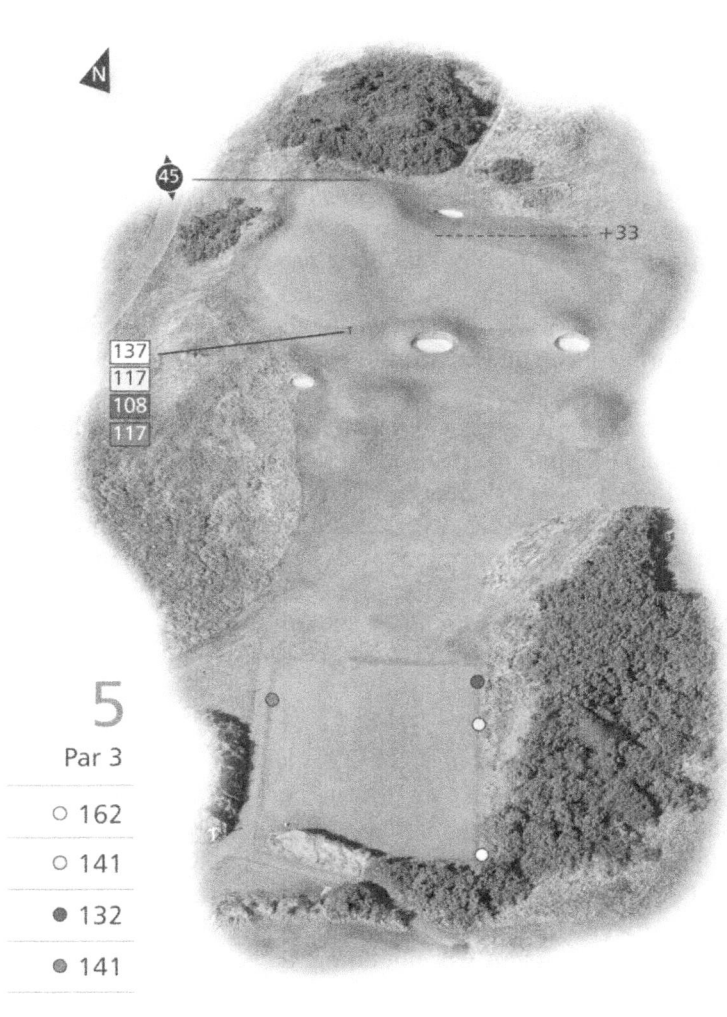

The fifth hole (Hackie's Barra) was a 162-yard par 3, with the pin on the lower level, guarded by two bunkers at the front. James watched Chris go through his preparations; reading the course booklet, checking the wind direction and thinking about which club to select. He was taking longer with his choice of club than he had on his other iron shots, and his face revealed some tension.

'Sorry about this, James. I am just trying to work out which club to go for here.'

'Don't worry about me, Chris. I would rather see a player take time to make the correct decision, than rush and either make a bad choice, or not be happy with the choice they make. Either of those outcomes will be a lot more frustrating than a little bit of a wait on the tee. More importantly though, Chris, do not waste time worrying about what your playing partners might be thinking. Your thinking processes should be 100 percent focused on helping you make the best decision and execute it with confidence. So, as I said, don't worry about me or anything else... just make your decision and commit to playing it.'

'Thanks, James. I don't know why I sometimes worry about what my playing partners might think– especially as they are usually trying to beat me! OK ... I'm good now, here we go.' Chris nodded to himself as if he was mentally checking off his decision and stepped forward confidently to the ball. He made a smooth swing with his selected iron and hit a low draw that bounced about fifteen feet to the left of the pin and rolled down the bank to rest about twenty-five feet behind the pin.

'Well, was that worth the wait, Chris?'

'I'm really happy with that shot, James, as that was basically what I was looking for. I was going to take my 6-iron, but I knew that it was the riskier shot, given that all the trouble is at the front. I, therefore, decided to go with the 5-iron and hit it into the bank. Going long was safer than short and I could use the bank to the left of the pin to bring the ball down to give me a straightish putt. Unfortunately, that is the sort of clear thinking that I am often guilty of not doing. It seems such an obvious thing to do – just take the safer option – that I don't know why I can't always do it. Even there, I was so close to just hitting the six; I don't even know why I started to second guess. Maybe you could tell me, as the expert?'

'Thanks for the compliment; but, to be honest, I think your description of the situation is a very good one. We sometimes don't give ourselves the space to think clearly and consider the risk-reward payoffs of a certain shot, even though this is one of the easiest ways to make a positive difference to your score. Golf is hard enough without making it harder. You took time to weigh up the risk and made a smart choice that allowed you to fully commit to what you were doing. You looked really confident as you approached the ball. How did it feel?'

'Once I stopped worrying about looking indecisive I actually felt good about my choice, and it is nice to know that I was "*doing sport psychology*". I really did feel good about the shot at the time and it has given me a boost to know that I can do the right thing.'

'Excellent! You should be proud of yourself. Sport psychology is all about giving yourself the best chance to get a good outcome and that is what you did. You took control of your thought processes and played the best shot for the situation. The more times you can do this in a round, the better your score will be.'

As Chris removed his putter from his bag, James fetched the flag. Chris still looked confident as he lined up his putt and made a good strike on his 25-footer, just to see it skim the right edge of the hole. He was still smiling as he tapped in for par.

Hole 6:
Playfair (498-yard par 5)

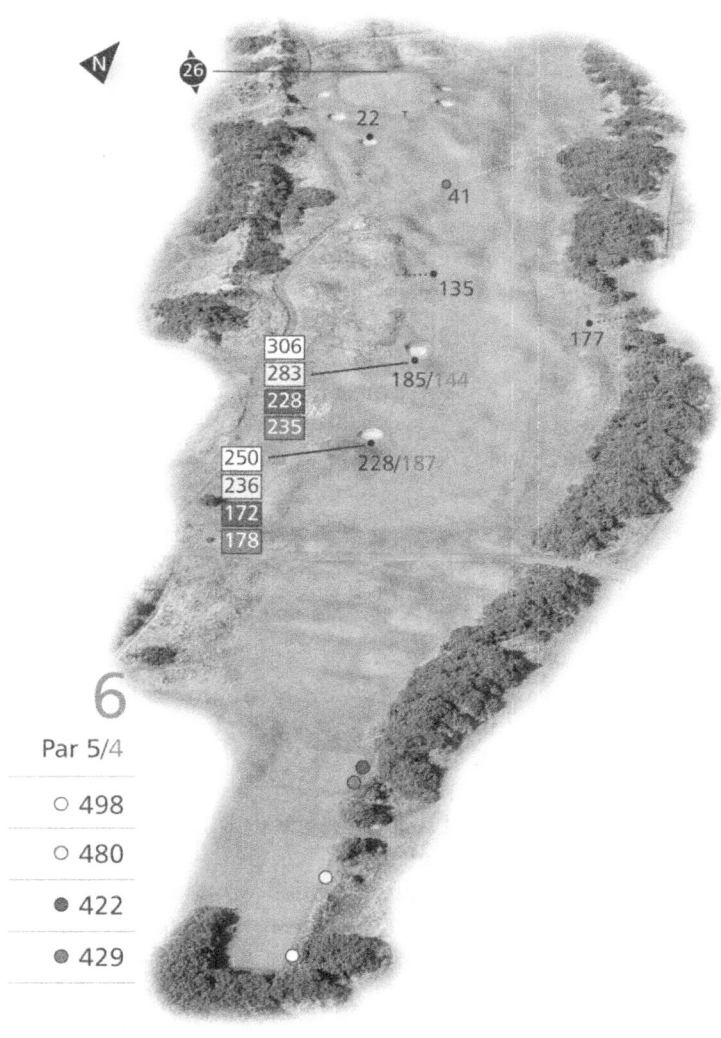

26

22

41

135

306
283
228
235

185/144

177

250
236
172
178

228/187

6

Par 5/4

○ 498

○ 480

● 422

● 429

The sixth hole was the toughest hole on the course; a challenging 498-yard par 5 with danger down the right-hand side off the tee and two fairway bunkers on the left side of the fairway. Before Chris teed off on this hole, James enquired about how he was feeling.

'I'm feeling good, quite well indeed.'

'I wonder what this feeling might mean for the hole you are about to play?'

Chris stopped for a moment, 'I think I know what you mean. Are you asking me whether my upbeat mood might affect what I think is going to happen on this hole?'

'Yes – that's right – I just wonder if you are using your feelings to determine the outcome of this hole and the score you would like to write in the scorecard when you finish.'

'Yes, that's exactly what I am thinking or – I suppose – feeling. This is usually how I think or feel my way round the golf course and there is often disaster lurking behind this way of feeling. I've tried to fight it in the past but the mirage ahead of me is too alluring.'

'I'm only asking this question because this is a par 5 with a stroke index 1. I wonder how you intend to play it? To help us out here, I'm going to ask you how you would play this hole if you were a Tour professional and then how *you* intend to play it.'

'I like that contrast. If I were a Tour professional, I guess I would play a 3-wood to the wide part of the fairway (about 280 yards off the tee), which would leave a 5-iron to the green (about 220 yards). A driver would bring in all the danger unless I was perfectly accurate with the drive. For me, I guess a 3-wood would get me to 240 yards off the tee, leaving me about 260 yards to the green. There is a wider section of the fairway about 120 yards from the green, which would leave me 150 yards with this second shot. I can hit my 9-iron 120 yards and my 7-iron 150 yards without forcing them. Just give me a second; I'll put my driver back in my bag. You know what, James, I feel strangely calm here with this 3-wood in my hands. I can hit it well most of the time and I know I've put my ego in the bag when I put my driver in there for this tee shot. I've been obsessed with distance and much less obsessed with a playing strategy that plays to my strengths. Let's see how I get on.'

James could see a complaisant side to Chris now. He was swinging his club freely as he performed his practice swings and there also seemed to be a more purposeful presence on the tee. Chris began his routine, stepped into the ball, glanced at his target a few times, and then smoothly swung back and through to a finish. The ball sailed down the centre of the fairway, bounced, and rolled out to the left-hand side about fifteen yards from the rough, between the two bunkers.

'Thanks, James. I'm glad you stopped me before I began that hole. I would have taken out my driver – in fact, I did take out my driver – I wasn't even stopping to think calmly about what was before me. My ball is where I would like it to be and I have my next two shots ahead to reach the green. Would you believe, I didn't really hit that 3-wood that hard; I certainly didn't force it.'

'Chris, who do you think is helping you play better golf?'

'I know it is me…but I also know that I am learning here as I go and that you are here with me. In that respect, I see how much you are influencing what I think, feel and do. Would you mind if we didn't speak until this hole is finished? I would just like to take the reins myself and see how I get on.' James agreed earnestly with this suggestion.

As Chris approached his ball he could see what lay ahead of him. It was curious to be here in this position on the fairway because it had rarely been the case in the past few months. It was as if he were playing someone else's ball. In fact, so strong was this conviction that it might be someone else's ball that he just checked his ball for his trademark red dots; and sure enough, it was his. He reached for his 7-iron, made two full practice swings, and stopped to see the flight of his ball in his mind's eye. Then he stepped into position, glanced three times at the target and then back to the ball, began his takeaway, and smoothly stroked the ball – finishing high, with his belt buckle facing the target. He held his finish until the ball bounced and stopped 110 yards from the green. He had outperformed himself in distance by reducing the demands he set upon himself. James remained about twenty yards behind and followed Chris as he cleaned his clubface thoroughly (first time in the round) and placed it discreetly into his bag and marched to his ball. He had 110 yards to the pin and because he had got his approach angle right, he was free to aim towards the pin between the bunkers protecting the left and right of the green.

Again, Chris began his routine as before. This distance was his true pitching-wedge distance (rather than the 130 yards he once hit during a bounce game which he told most people about when they asked him how far he hit his pitching wedge). He stroked the ball as he had on his previous wedge shot and the ball fired high into the air, looking straight down the flag, stopping just over the flag and rolling a few feet to stop. He was left with a seven-foot putt for birdie. James watched Chris walk to the green and leave his bag just off the side in the direction of the seventh tee. He slipped off the putter head cover and meticulously repaired the pitch mark.

A four-ball at the next tee witnessed his approach shot and were eagerly awaiting the putt. With the audacious approach shot, they imagined it must have been a birdie putt. Chris removed the pin, marked his ball and cleaned it (first time in the round), placing the line on the ball on his intended line for his putt. He stood up, made a practice stroke, and made his putt. The ball rolled straight, with a little deviation towards the end, and dropped into the cup. Chris exchanged the flag for his ball and stepped off to the side, waiting for James.

'So how did that hole go for you, Chris?'

'What?' said Chris disbelievingly. 'Did you not see it?'

'Did I not see what?'

'My birdie,' responded Chris in amazement.

'Oh yes, I saw what happened but I asked you how did that hole go for you, Chris.' Chris was annoyed with this question. Wasn't the answer obvious? It was golf at its best. What the hell does he mean with his *'how did that hole go for you?'* This is the psychological mumbo jumbo that I can't stand. No wonder this psychobabble gets such a bad name.

'I feel like you are playing a game with me here and I don't like it. I chose the club that was best for the yardage; I didn't overestimate my ability. I made my practice swings, pictured the shot I wanted and smoothly stroked the ball to my target. I didn't force anything and walked off with a birdie and you're asking me, "How did that hole go for you, Chris?" '

There was a pause for a few moments; then James broke the silence, 'I see that you are annoyed with my question but my intention was not to annoy you. What I wanted to know was whether you felt that the outcome on this hole was something you could accept without feeling it didn't fit the image of yourself. Some golfers see themselves as someone who scores 5 over par or 8 over par. Having scored a birdie on one hole, for example, a golfer with this self-image finds a way of dealing with this discomfort – of playing better than usual – by bogeying or double bogeying the next hole, playing worse than, or at least the same as, usual.'

'OK, I see what you mean. What you are saying is that although I might be happy with my birdie now, after a few moments I'll try to figure out why I scored a birdie and be left with a dilemma: either I am ready to accept that I can play golf well or I am not ready to accept it. You know, that point makes a lot of sense to me now. I guess I would like to think I am a good golfer; but when I play golf well, I continually discount what I have done. In fact, a few weeks ago I birdied two holes in a row and all I could think about on the next hole was, "What the hell is going on here – I'm two under after four holes?" It was an unsettling feeling and when I double bogeyed the next two holes, I found myself back in my comfortable slot.'

'We all live with an image we have created about ourselves – our self-image. It becomes an accepted image and being that person, with that image, is a regretful place to be. Although it may be annoying and frustrating at times, it doesn't require any change. And change can be too scary and painful for some people. They come to a crossroads and it seems easier to turn back, rather than go through the challenging process of change.'

'So are you asking me if I am ready to change? Am I ready to change the image I have of myself as a golfer? I suppose I'm not sure.' 'That's OK, Chris; remember that what we are talking about here is not just for the here and now; it's for the next few months until you get what you want from our work together. We cannot demand instant change but what we can do is ensure you have all the elements you need to change and to maintain the changes you forge. If you are patient, open to learning and change, you will get what you want from our work together.'

'I think I can answer your question now…that was one hell of a tough hole!' And they both laughed as they walked to the seventh tee.

By now Chris was gaining a new perspective on himself and his golf game.

Hole 7:
Ayton (373-yard par 4)

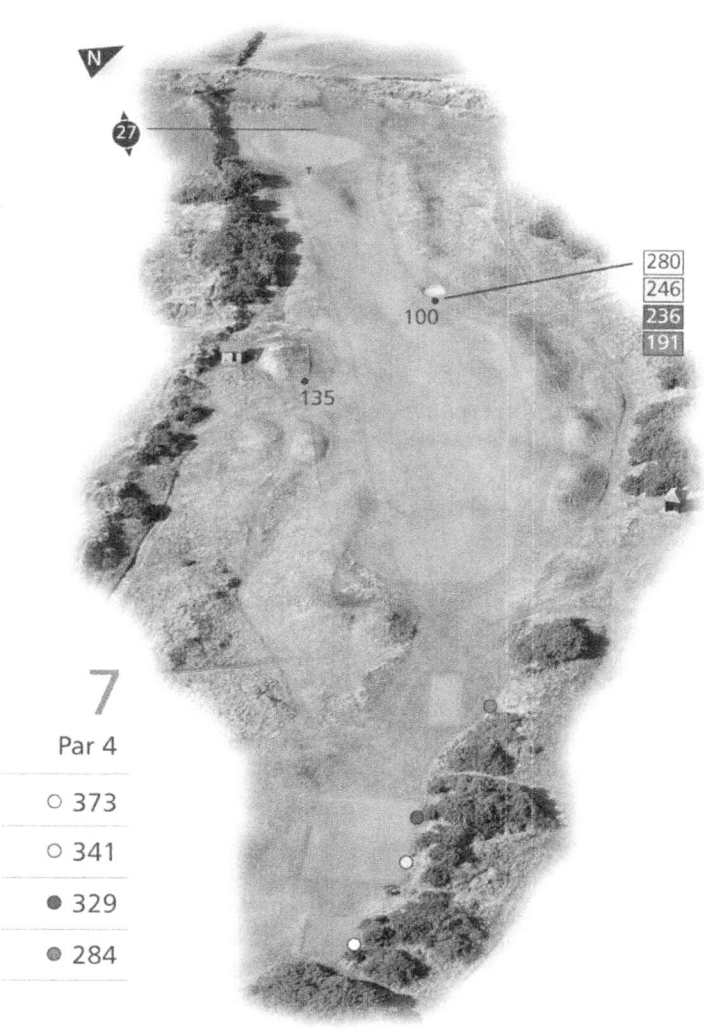

'You know, James, I'm just realising something,' Chris explained, as he beamed with delight at his own insight to himself. 'I'm realising that I have been holding onto a dreadful image of myself as a golfer. And not only do I hold that image of myself as a golfer, but maybe of myself also; I seek every opportunity to confirm that "I'm bad" in some way. I played a few good rounds last year during August and I explained it all away as a stroke of luck – a bit of good fortune. But, really, I was trying to get myself off the hook of having to live up to the standards of good golf – can you explain that to me?'

There seemed like there was some time available to them because the fourball behind were not on the tee yet, so James began to tell a story about a player he had met a few years ago. 'Chris, let me tell you a story about a golfer I met two years ago. I met this golfer – let's just call him John for now – just like we are meeting here. He wanted me to come out on the course with him and "put his game right". In fact, he wanted me to "get him sorted for the year ahead". I guessed at the time what he was aiming towards but I wasn't certain. Let's just say he had a chance of making it on the European Tour full-time because he had been on the Tour twice before, for a year at a time, but then dropped down to the Challenge Tour for the intervening years. All in all, it seemed like a frustrating time for him.

I walked round the eighteen holes with him – quite a leisurely game, at least for the first twelve holes. It was an exhibition of ball striking and exquisite short game skills. Now that I think about it, I guess he must have been 5 under par by the 12th. And then, as if out of nowhere, someone else was there. I couldn't believe what I was seeing. This calm, relaxed and confident golfer was giving way to a jittery, uptight and fearful golfer in the space of a few minutes. The drive on the 13th hole landed in the rough on the right-hand side about 10 yards off the fairway. The talking finished – the enjoyable leisurely discussion was over. There was silence, apart from a few choice words after the drive. John's caddie and I walked down the fairway as John walked ahead alone, veering toward his ball in the rough. His caddie said, "Do you remember I mentioned the other guy I caddy for – well, that's him, and I wasn't sure if he would be here today with nothing at stake; but hey, here he is. Oh, best of luck!"

From the 13th hole to the 18th, he dropped seven shots. One dropped at the 13th, 14th, 15th, a double at the 16th and a bogey at 17 and 18. He had a face like thunder and it was almost impossible to speak with him.

His caddie, Mike, wasn't enjoying the experience either and confided that, "We've been through a lot together but I'm not sure what I can do for him anymore. He's a top lad, you know – he'd give you his last crust of bread – but he's ruining himself out here."

I gave John time after the round to shower and suggested we sit down for a while to talk. I asked John what it was about himself that he most admired. It took him quite a while to answer and eventually he said, half-choked with tears: "I don't know…I'm not sure…not sure if there is anything." After a long pause, John gathered himself and said, "There are things that I know I should say about myself; there are things that I am but I see grey when there shouldn't be grey. I'm fighting this demanding demon inside me and he's winning, you know, he's beating me down. I'm a positive person but when I'm on the golf course or at the range it's as if there is another person holding the club and I'm not there. I'm exhausted from fighting this guy – absolutely exhausted."

We spoke for a few hours that evening. John led the session, talking about himself and his girlfriend, his mum, his dad, his coach, and his brother. He talked about what it felt like to be him as a person and as someone who played golf for a living. He didn't just tell me this story in words, he told me in feelings. He said he couldn't accept himself as anything less than perfect. I remember the silence after I said to him: "When your idea of normal is everyone around you approving of you and your golf all the time, you've set the bar too high – too high; you'll never clear it with those demands." He said, "Can you say that to me again – I need to record it on my phone?" And so I did.

We began to work closely – week after week, for three months. John had done his utmost to ensure he would never play his best golf. It was a long way back but he began to realise who he was and to accept himself as a fallible human being – someone who made mistakes. The work John put into learning about himself and learning to treat himself better has paid off handsomely and I'm not just talking financially. He respects himself as a person and as a golfer. John learned to check the accuracy of his thoughts by searching for distortions. He also began to think about what his thoughts made him feel and do. He started to think about his values and whether such thoughts were helping him to realise them.'

'Wow, that's some story,' Chris said. 'I never thought the players on Tour would be like that but I guess they're human too – fallible human beings – I like that because it makes me feel a whole lot better.'

41

After another nice hybrid from the tee on the par 4 seventh, Chris walked confidently towards his ball, placed perfectly on the right half of the fairway. He had been quiet since the tee shot but as he neared the ball, he turned round to James.

'I have been thinking more about John's story and what it means for me. I know that it is common sense, really, but it was important for me to hear you tell it, James. I am not going to be perfect, on the golf course … or anywhere, for that matter. I just have to do my best and not get in my own way. I know it sounds stupid, but knowing that even top players sometimes tie themselves up in knots thinking like that, is a bit like … I don't know … like a sort of fog has lifted and I can see clearly. I have always beaten myself up for having these weak thoughts and that just makes things worse, so I beat myself up some more and on it goes. It is obvious that I should give myself a break and make it easier to play, but maybe it took hearing it from someone else to make me believe it. It's only a game after all, and while it might be important to me to do well, I shouldn't let it control my moods like I do. I feel I am a different golfer already. Does this mean I am *cured,* James? Can we walk in now and I only have to pay you half?!'

'Thanks for the kind words, Chris; I'm really enjoying our time together as well. I'm also glad that John's story resonated with you and helped you question the way you talk to yourself. In fact, I really liked the way you put it with your "fog lifting" metaphor. Do you mind if I "steal" that? Playing golf in fog would be difficult and scary, as you would not know where the danger is; would have to keep second-guessing what you should do; and your imagination would go wild thinking about what could go wrong. When it lifts you can just play what is there – there are no hidden fears. Playing with your mind full of negative thoughts is like playing in fog – and, just like no golf course would let you play in fog, you should not let yourself play with a foggy mind.'

'Wow, that sounds great. It's nice for me to know that my muddled thoughts actually make sense. It would be cool to think you might talk about my "foggy mind" with other golfers. Maybe some other poor sod out there might feel a bit better after hearing my story, the way I did when I heard John's. Anyway, I guess I had better get on with the golf then, and smack this ball by that pin.'

Chris' mid-iron approach shot drew right into the back left corner of the green, running up to ten feet from the flag.

'That was one of the best feeling shots I have ever played. I just felt so comfortable over the ball. It was like part of my brain was still thinking about our conversation on fog lifting while another part was sort of watching me getting on with the golf shot in autopilot. How do you explain that, James? I thought I should not let myself be distracted, yet it felt really great there.'

'I like the way you are being aware of your thoughts at the moment without letting them become too intrusive. That is one of the secrets of a good mental game, so well done with that. To be honest, there are no hard and fast rules about swing thoughts – some golfers use quite a few while others like to let their minds go blank. The main thing is that you feel comfortable and don't let your thoughts compete with each other, or start to interfere with how you make your swing. It sounds as though your thoughts were all just happening naturally and were helping you feel relaxed and confident. You looked really relaxed there and if you were not thinking about the swing itself, that would explain why it would have felt like it was in autopilot. So, I would not be worried about having two sets of thoughts like that. In fact, it sounds like it helped create a perfect state for you to swing.'

'Yeah, I loved it… While I still have this positive mindset, and before I start worrying about how I'm going to keep this up, I'm gonna go ahead and hole this putt.'

The ball never looked like going anywhere but the centre of the hole and Chris had just made two birdies in a row.

'Get in there!'

Hole 8:
Eden's Edge (369-yard par 4)

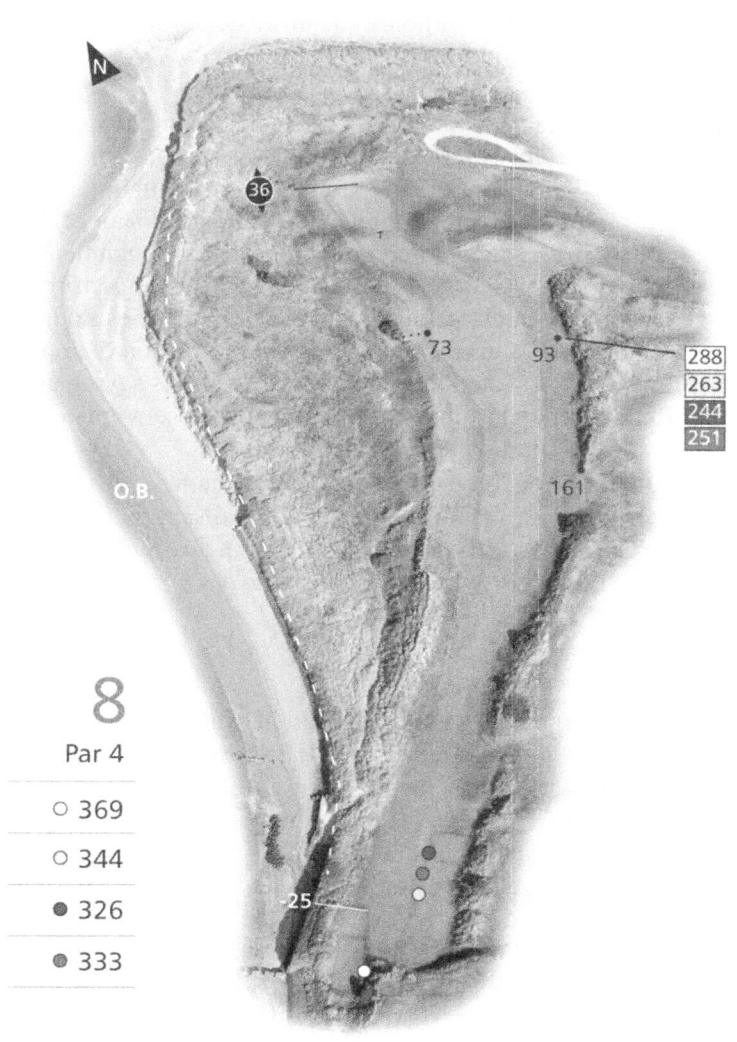

8
Par 4

○ 369
○ 344
● 326
● 333

288
263
244
251

O.B.

36

73

93

161

-25

The eighth hole is a 369-yard par 4 with a relatively tight fairway running alongside the sand of the Eden Estuary, but with a generous green. James felt Chris focused on impressing other golfers, rather than upon the task before him and it would take time working on his game before this issue could be amended. Earlier in the round Chris had mentioned the feelings of shame he felt – especially, in the clubhouse – after a game, if he had played poorly. James wished to explore this strong, and often disruptive, emotion with Chris. Although he had played exquisitely for the last couple of holes, the influence of unhelpful emotions perhaps bubbled just below this calm surface.

Chris' tee shot was long and straight but carried further than he expected, into the rough on the right-hand side of the fairway. It was a mixture of emotions for Chris. First, James could see him jut his chin out as he held his finish at the top of his swing – it looked like the ideal shot off the tee but once it hit the fairway it continued into the rough – rough that would impede a decent approach shot to the green. Once his eyes confirmed that the ball was in the rough, he deflated. And before James said anything, Chris jumped to his own defence: 'From position A to position Z in two seconds.' Chris' intention was to prevent James saying anything that might offend him, by hitting himself first with those words.

As Chris and James meandered down the fairway, James said deliberately, 'Ah, that's a shame,' referring to the disappointed expectation on Chris' part. Chris didn't speak for a few moments, then said; 'You know, that's just what my dad used to say.'

James enquired, 'That's a shame?'

'Yes, those exact words. He never really said he was disappointed with me but he didn't need to. I could hear it in the words he used – "that's a shame" or, as I saw it, "I'm ashamed of you". If I didn't do well in school exams he'd say, "Ah, that's a pity; you're such a smart boy", and I know he probably meant well, but those words cut me to the bone. I'd let him down again. But, as I saw it, I always let him down. I wanted to be a better student for Dad's sake; I wanted to be a better golfer for Dad's sake. I wanted to show him I was worth something and I could do that if I did things well, you know? Even now, when I call home and he asks how things are at work or whatever, I'd want to tell the best story possible so that he'd be proud of me. I know this all probably sounds crazy to you. Does it sound crazy to you, James?"

'I think what's important is how it sounds to you. Does it sound right to you?'

'Yes... yes, I suppose it does. I've got to tell you, James, that's a wall of tears I haven't got over yet. I remember one time we went out to play a round of golf. I'd say I was probably fourteen years old at the time and... boy, I was playing well. It was a beautiful summer's evening and Dad was home early from work, and I pleaded with Dad to get nine holes in before teatime. We headed down to the course and I had one of the games of my life – I was flushing it. I could see my dad – he was swelling with pride. He'd never say it but, as you psychologists say, it was "leaking" out. I was two under at the turn and it was getting close to teatime, and Mum would want us back. But I was going so well I didn't want to stop. I'd never broken par around the course and maybe, just maybe, if I kept going I'd do it. Dad was adamant we go home for tea but I could also see he wanted to see me break par on the course. When we came in off the ninth, Dad ran to the clubhouse as I started to clean my shoes and get ready to go. But he came out about two minutes later and said we're good to go. I knew he must have rung Mum to say we'd be late.

I asked Dad what he had said to mum. He said, "Some things in life are so precious you just can't miss them for anything". I didn't know what he was talking about at the time but I do now. I think he was enjoying seeing me so happy, doing what I loved, playing the best game in the world. The back nine started like the front nine. I was flushing it. I dropped a shot on the 12th and 15th. And I three putted the 16th to put me one over with two holes to play – the two holes with the highest stroke index on the card. I made birdie at the par three 17th and I needed a birdie at 18 to break par at the course. The 18th was 405 yards and, at fourteen years old, I struggled a lot on this hole. I hit a good drive but I still had a long way to go to reach the green. Funnily enough, I remember saying to myself as I walked down the fairway, "I'm going to do it" – over and over again. When I got to my ball, I pulled out my 5-iron and hit the sweetest shot of my life – you know when you just know – yeah, it was one of them. The clubhouse is just beside the 18th green, and everyone in the restaurant and bar can see you. My ball had pitched at the mouth of the green and run out to the flag, stopping six feet with a slight uphill putt. I tell you, I was shaking when I saw the putt I had to finish the game. No one in the clubhouse or restaurant knew what this putt meant – nobody knew except Dad and me. Someone had just finished ahead of us and shouted out, "Is it for birdie?" I said, "Yeah" –

then he said, "No pressure, then?" I didn't answer. I just let Dad finish his putt and I stroked my ball into the centre of the cup.

We both knew what I had just done but, trying to be like my dad, I didn't say anything. I wanted him to think that this was just the start and I could be so much better. Dad never said too much. Definitely no boasting allowed in our house. But as we walked off the green he said, "I've played and seen lots of golf – great memories, great days. I saw Watson beat Nicklaus at Turnberry a few weeks after you were born. I saw Seve win at St Andrews in '84, do you remember? Do you remember the fist pumps? Absolutely terrific days.......let's go to the Open this year." I said, "Ah, brilliant Dad!" That was Dad for you, no praise. It was like it never happened.

When we got home, Mum said, "How did you get on?" I said, "Oh, fine," not letting on. I was bursting to tell her – but as usual, I was stifling those emotions. I wanted Dad to tell her. I wanted Dad to be proud of me. But you know – he never did. Or at least, not while I was there; he came in and asked, "What's for tea?"

But you know, Dad kept a diary – crazy, I know, who keeps a diary? He wouldn't say much but he used to write in his diary, and last year I was clearing out some cupboards for Mum and I came across the diary for 1991. And I know I shouldn't have been looking at his diary but I was eager to see if he wrote anything. I knew the date 17th June 1991. There were just a few words there – nothing else, just a few words. "Spent the evening with Chris – best day of my life." He couldn't tell me, and I always thought he was proud of me that day; and I know – in his own way, he was. You know, I welled up when I read that entry.'

Chris paused for a moment – he had reached his ball and saw how it lay in the rough. 'Time to switch on, James – it's time to switch on.'

Chris spent some time preparing for this shot. It was a short wedge to the green and if he played it conservatively he would leave himself a good putt for birdie. Chris made a fine attempt towards the green but the ball ran off the back – it had come out "hot". He two putted and walked off with a par. James and Chris didn't say anything for a while. James just wanted Chris to enjoy the journey out on the course. James knew the intensity of the story that Chris has just relayed – the love of a parent for his child and a child for his parent. Golf is never simply about golf. It's about all the good things in life – family, friends, love, honesty, loyalty and hard work.

When Chris walked to the next tee, James asked Chris, 'How are you feeling?'

'You know, James, I'm feeling proud and maybe I just need to be a little better to myself more of the time – it's what my parents would want for me and it's what I want for myself. This round of golf is more about my life than it is about my golf. I think that's funny.'

'It is funny, Chris; golf is just one of those things we choose to do to express ourselves. And I guess that's what we are trying to do. We are trying to express ourselves to other people. People we care about and people who care about us.'

Hole 9:
Windy tap (192-yard par 3)

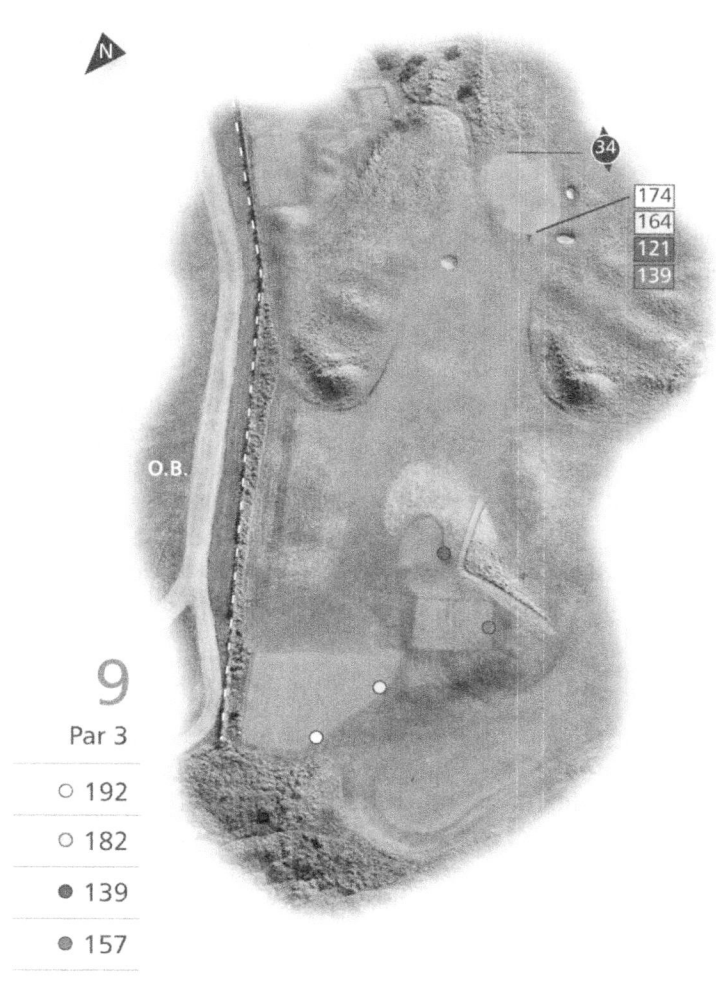

9
Par 3

○ 192
○ 182
● 139
● 157

The funny thing about opening up to the possibility that we can be a little better to ourselves is that once that genie is let out, it is hard to stuff it back in the bottle again. This does not mean that we are dampening our competitive fire, but rather, removing some of the additional sources of unnecessary pressure that can build up … 'I must be perfect'; 'I want to make "them" proud'; 'I don't want to let "them" down'. Instead of focusing on what might be at stake if we don't meet expectations, it is more likely that we will keep our focus on enjoying the moment and responding to the challenges that golf provides. For Chris, the current challenge was trying to find the putting surface, 192 yards away on this tricky par 3.

'Well, I am not going to let these positive thoughts go to waste, James. I am going to thread this 4-iron right between those bunkers there.' After a confident swing, the ball did draw beautifully through the gap at the front of the green but ran on through the green to lie in the light rough off the back.

'Hold on…hold on…awh, come on! Do you know what, James? That was my favourite shot of the round so far. In fact, I can't remember the last time I felt so certain about a shot. I absolutely saw that ball flight in advance and it felt kinda like I was hitting repeat on a video. It was like when I was a kid and I just played shots that I wanted to see, without any fear of what might happen. That felt so damn good.'

'It was a lovely strike, Chris. You looked so loose and calm there. Perhaps, I am getting a glimpse of what you would have looked like when you played with your dad. Enjoying each shot for what it is – a chance to express yourself?'

'Maybe I am. I just know that I used to love the chance to play the more difficult shots just to see if I could do it. I had that confidence to go for things and not care about what happened. Is it just part of growing up that we start to think about what we have at stake if we muck things up?'

'Well, it is true that we often don't play in the same way as adults; and I mean "play" in the "playground" sense, just mucking about, enjoying the experience for what it is – fun – not an occasion to be judged. As the saying goes, "We don't stop playing because we grow old. We grow old because we stop playing!" '

'Ha ha. I like that. It is true in my case, though. Golf has increasingly stopped being the escape from the daily grind that it used to be. It has become another part of the daily grind – another chance for me to show my faults and weaknesses and my waste of talent. I think that is why talking about my dad was so powerful for me on the last hole. Rather than waste energy worrying about how he or others might judge me as a golfer and a person, I guess I should just focus on enjoying the experience of playing golf – like I used to.'

'I think that is a great idea. Do you think you would play a shot differently with a smile on your face and thinking about the challenge of executing the skill, compared to if you were upset about the outcome of the previous shot and worried about what might happen if you make another bad shot?'

'Oh, definitely! I mean, even just now, I am proud – and a little surprised – at how I wasn't upset after the tee shot – where it ended up. I know I would have been, earlier in the round. Instead, I was able to hold on to the pleasure I took in the feeling of confidence I had before the shot and the feeling of executing it perfectly, like I had imagined. Of course, I would rather be on the green – putting for birdie – but I feel fortunate that I got to have those great feelings before the shot and I want to continue to keep enjoying my shots like that if I can.

On that note – here we are. Right, if I was playing for fun and with confidence, I would probably try to flop this up onto the top level there. So … let's do it.'

Chris lobbed the ball up onto the level and it stopped within three feet of its first bounce, right on the lip of the hole.

'Excellent shot, Chris. That was beautifully played.'

'Thanks, James. It just felt like the right shot and I think you are right that I probably played it with a smile on my face. Usually, I would still be trying to deal with my feelings of unfairness after the tee shot, and worrying about getting a bogey after thinking I would be on for a birdie while my tee shot was in the air. It's always nice to be able to tap in the ball with the wedge and not have to get the putter out. Mind you, I enjoyed the previous two shots even more, as I played them with such feel and confidence. I had no doubts whatsoever … no voice in my head telling me to be careful. I just did what I wanted to do … what I know I am capable of doing if I can just get out of my own way.'

'Yes, I was impressed by the way you dealt with that hole. It would have been easy to have got upset about the tee shot and make hard work of the chip back. Instead, you trusted yourself and played the shots that you wanted. I am really enjoying watching this side of you, Chris. Lock in these feelings, and remember what it is like to feel this free.'

Hole 10:
Spires (411 yards par 4)

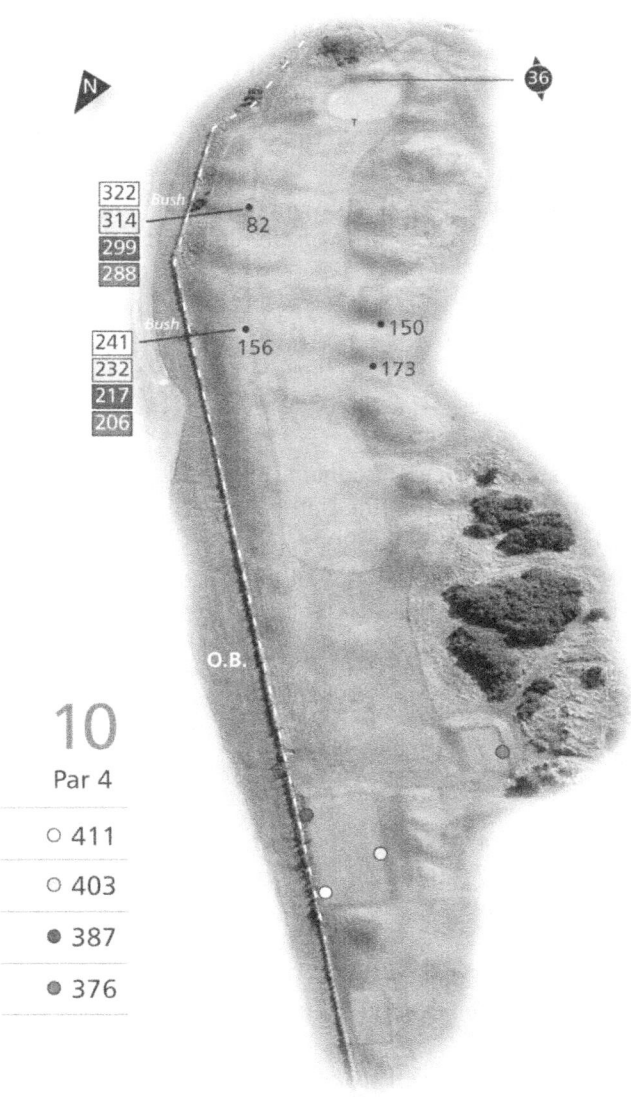

322	Bush
314	82
299	
288	

241	Bush
232	156
217	
206	

150
173

O.B.

10
Par 4

○ 411
○ 403
● 387
● 376

As James and Chris sauntered to the 10th tee, Chris asked:

'Do I look like a 4-handicap golfer to you?'

'I guess what I am hearing is that you don't feel like you are a 4-handicap golfer?'

'Exactly – look at what I have just done on the front nine – that's how I know I can play golf. That golfer is inside, but I can't let him loose.'

'I sense you are afraid of letting him loose in case of what he might do.'

'Yeah, I suppose I don't trust him. I've damned him and shouted at him and cursed him, and maybe I don't think he can do the job of playing golf,'

'How is that golfer inside you doing today?'

Chris chuckled, 'Good, I guess. I just need to find a way to trust him.'

'You know, Chris, it sounds to me like that voice inside you is like a critical parent controlling and manipulating that golfer within you. From what you said earlier, you "shouted at him and cursed him". I just wonder if you are afraid to let that inner child grow up – maybe you are protecting him from the hurt and pain. The inner child, or what I call "my seven-year-old self" needs support, encouragement, kindness and patience. Can you do something for me while we have a minute here? Can you remember when you were seven?'

'Yeah – I can.'

'Well, what I would like you to do is tell me what you would like to say to your "seven-year-old self" now. How would you like to speak to him and what would you like to say?'

Chris paused for a while and then said playfully, 'What are you trying to do to me, James? Should I be lying on a couch?'

Chris was trying to distance himself from the feelings that were beginning to wash over him – potent and threatening as they seemed to him. James persisted and enquired sensitively, 'Is this difficult for you –

maybe even painful? Perhaps, because of the hurt you feel now, you wish to protect your "seven-year-old self" from the pain you know.'

'Yes,' murmured Chris, 'I want to tell him he's a good lad and he deserves respect. And his big heart is nothing to be ashamed of; and just because he feels things, he shouldn't run away from those feelings or hide them because they will make him be something he is not. I want to tell him that if he is sad he can cry, and if he is happy he can be happy, and if he wants to be silly he can be silly! And I want to say to him that a fucking golf ball should not make him feel that he is any less of a person because it doesn't go where he wants it to go. He doesn't feel he is any good and he tries so hard but it's never enough.'

There was a silence for a minute and Chris spoke again.

'Sorry about the language, James.'

'Chris, I felt your sadness and guilt for the child inside, who had such a hard time. That forgotten child within was struggling to perform to someone else's standards.'

Chris nodded in agreement.

'I feel you could spend some time with that child inside – the forgotten child – to help him feel better; maybe to help him feel a little less guilty and a little more love and freedom. With time and patience, you can help to remove the guilt and self-doubt for that child inside. With time and patience, you can help develop a calm and confident feeling where there once was insecurity, blame and self-doubt.'

'You know, James, I could run away from what we just did there. I could run away and hide from it. It was powerful, maybe even too powerful for me – a huge wave of anger and resentment and sadness and guilt – oh, the guilt! And I wanted to push it away, put it back into the box and get as far away from it as possible – do you understand?'

James nodded to indicate his understanding.

'I've been hiding from those emotions – maybe all emotions all my life. I thought I wasn't supposed to feel. So that's just what I did. There's a lump in my throat just saying this stuff. I remember one time after a breakup with a girl I was seeing, a friend of mine said, "How come nothing ever seems to bother you? You don't seem to feel anything. I would be broken right now."

But I was lying, wasn't I? I was pretending. Just like that song by Freddie Mercury, "The Great Pretender", and that line, "I seem to be what I'm not, you see".'

At this time, Chris was teeing up the ball. He got set up and lashed at the ball. The ball left the clubface and soared like an arrow; it seemed to travel for an age in the air. They saw it land, then bounce and run. There was a slight breeze behind, too. But the ball came to rest 80 yards or so from the green – a drive of 331 yards.

'Wow – that's one hell of a drive, Chris!'

'There was some emotion in there – and I don't know if it was anger or relief, James.'

As they walked and talked down the fairway, Chris appeared loose, chatty and happy. He hit his wedge to fifteen feet and two putted for par. As James placed the flagstick in the ground, Chris said, 'I feel like I've lost a stone weight off myself. I mean off my shoulders. I really enjoyed what we talked about back there. In fact, I didn't even concentrate on that wedge into the green because I was thinking about that "forgotten child" and that image of me at seven years old is striking.'

'Chris, we've pulled a few weeds in the garden and it's looking better. With patience and care we'll get that garden back in full bloom.'

'I like that metaphor – Dr Titchmarsh.'

James laughed out loud and Chris joined him. Chris was happy to see that James could laugh heartily and he thought to himself, 'He's alright – I like him. He cares; he cares about me.'

Hole 11:
Treble One (497-yard par 5)

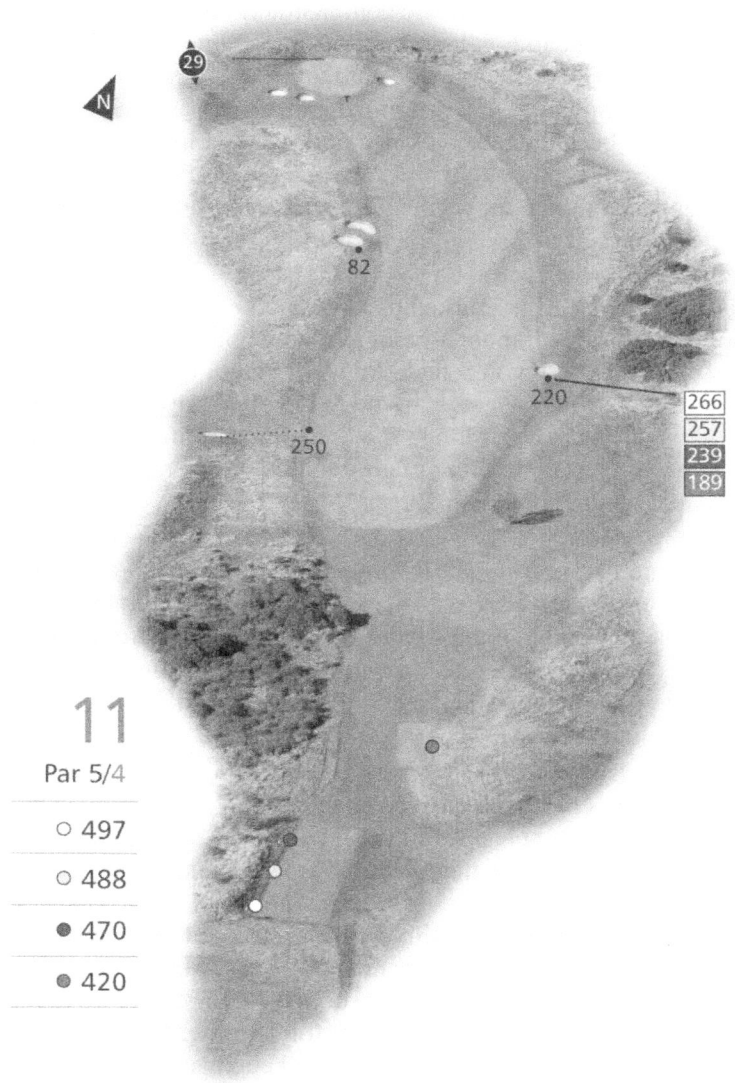

29

N

82

220

250

266
257
239
189

11

Par 5/4

○ 497

○ 488

● 470

● 420

Although Chris' drive on the 11th was not as well-struck as on the 10th, it managed to cling onto the left-hand side of the fairway after it drew a little more than he had allowed for. James was interested to note that Chris' demeanour before, during and after making his swing was now more relaxed and he did not look like the same nervous ball of energy on the tee as he had earlier in the round. Even though he still watched carefully as his ball headed towards the left-hand semi-rough on the wind, there was not the same manic commentary. Part of this change was, undoubtedly, due to him being more comfortable being the focus of James' 'scrutiny'. However, it was clear that he was also more comfortable playing under his own, much more severe, scrutiny – a scrutiny that had been unbalanced, unsupportive and impossible to live up to. For James, this process of working to a place of self-acceptance was more important than improving golf cards or holing more putts. It had a more lasting effect.

As he left the tee box, Chris turned to James, 'I've been thinking about how good I feel at the moment – being out here, playing on this cracking golf course, talking with you. I feel like I belong out here. This is exactly where I am supposed to be at the moment. Do you know what I mean? I have spent what seems like a long time dreading certain shots, certain holes – hell, even just competing in golf at all. I wonder now why the hell I bothered lacing up my spikes.'

'It sounds to me like you are allowing yourself to be happy out here. You trust yourself to play the shots and accept the consequences as they unfold. It's like you said on the last hole – you need to learn to trust the golfer within you and let him get on with the job of playing golf while you step back, offer support, and enjoy the experience.'

'Yeah – I guess I've never been a good passenger. I'm like the worst sort of backseat driver; criticising and complaining, but not helping at all. I see that. I just wait for a chance to jump in and criticise while "the driver" can't relax, knowing that the mistake will undoubtedly come, that will result in the negative comment. The image of my father comes into my head too when I think about this – he only seemed to comment when there was something to criticise. Or, make sure that I knew that a chance to let him down might just be round the corner – "Sure, you've played the front nine well son, but it won't count for anything if you muck up the back nine." Basically, I have managed to keep that judgmental side of my dad alive, while I still try to play golf like the child looking for praise, but knowing that he will not live up to what is expected. Christ! How messed up is that?!'

'It's not messed up at all, Chris. It's a perfectly understandable reaction, given the complicated relationship between you, golf and your father. I think that you have been incredibly brave to grapple with these issues and I am proud of you for the insights you have developed. Think of the new language you are developing for your golf game. I have listened to you talk about "enjoyment" and "confidence" and "trust" in the last few holes. This is not the language of someone who is waiting to assess and criticise and demean. It is the language of growth and support and acceptance. You are changing your internal commentary to a more positive one.'

'Hmmm. It certainly seems like a nicer commentary to listen to. I guess it is not surprising that I would feel better with a supportive, rather than a judgmental, soundtrack to my round.'

Almost incidentally, Chris had selected a long iron while speaking and settled into his pre-shot routine. The ball flew straight and landed on the right-hand side of the fairway, about eighty yards from the green – the perfect angle to attack the pin. After taking a few purposeful steps towards his ball, Chris slowed up and walked over towards James.

'James, although things are going well at the moment, I guess I have been down on myself for too long to just think that this is it. Perhaps it is just the pessimist in me but I guess I am still worried that the old voice will re-emerge. What will I do then? It's easy with you here, guiding me, prompting me, but what if I can't manage on my own?'

'You will cope just fine, Chris,' said James warmly. 'Of course, you will sometimes have difficult times on the golf course, but the important thing is not to beat yourself up. Give yourself space to grow and learn, and try and enjoy the ride. You deserve a positive soundtrack to your golf – and your life – and only you can provide it.'

Chris seemed satisfied, for now, with James' response and settled into his routine for his pitch shot. His wedge shot was caught a bit thin and ran twenty feet past the pin, towards the back of the green.

'Not my best, James, but long was always the safer option with the three bunkers guarding the front of the green. Maybe I thought a little too much about them and let it affect my swing.'

Turning to face James, he added, 'I can live with that, though.' A good long putt left Chris with just over two feet to clean up for another par.

Hole 12:
The Butts (538-yard par 5)

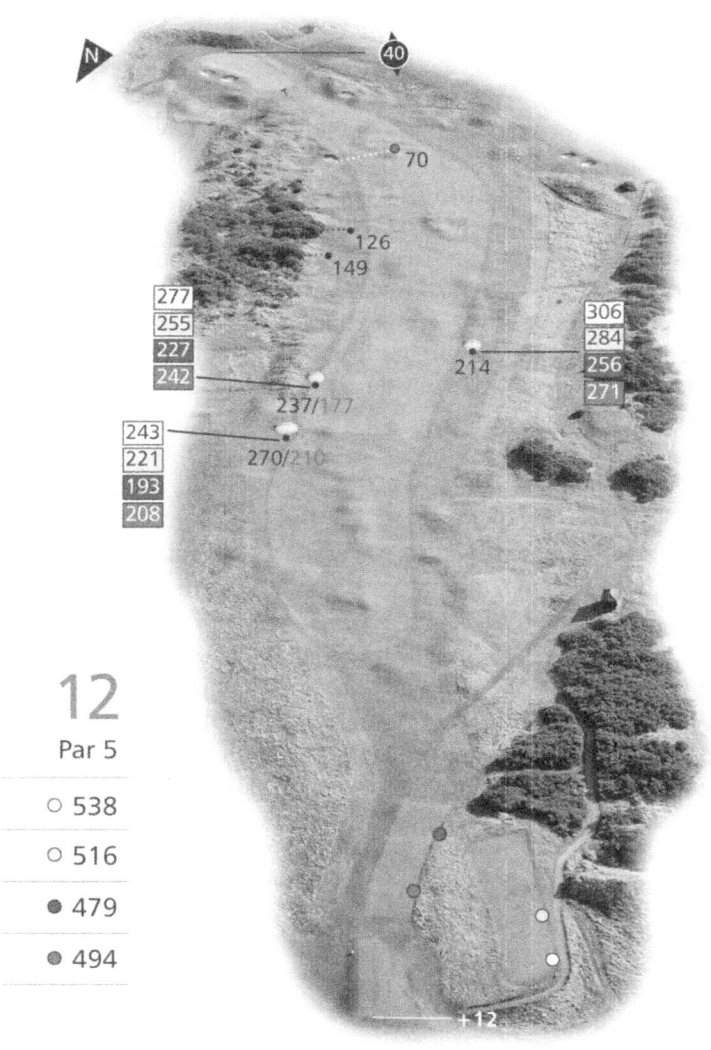

12

Par 5

○ 538

○ 516

● 479

● 494

As Chris and James rambled to the 12th tee, Chris put his hand on James' shoulder and said, 'Thanks, James; thank you very much, indeed.'

James replied with an emphatic, 'I haven't hit one shot out here today.' James' intention was to help Chris to see that Chris was helping himself, not James.

'Yes, I guess you haven't hit any shots but, somehow, I feel I'm playing better golf because of you.'

'You know, Chris, we've been talking and listening to each other for the past hour and half. I've enjoyed it. I've enjoyed getting to know you, Chris – as a person, and as a golfer. But we can only get to know each other and work well together when we trust each other. Part of building that trust is for us to be honest. I feel you want to give me more credit than I deserve out here. Perhaps I had some small role to play but I need to emphasise that it is you who are in charge. I am here to support you but you are in charge. You are in the driver's seat and I am in the passenger's seat. The reins of your destiny are in your hands – not in mine.'

'But haven't you helped me here today? I've learned a lot about myself and I know I am going to learn more. I'm beginning to understand that liking and accepting myself is possible and I'm on that journey. And if we are being honest, why are you not accepting my thanks?'

'It is a true pleasure to help people and it's a major reason why I do what I do. And I appreciate your kindness towards me; however, there is a trap I can fall into here too. I can begin to think that golfers' improving is all about me. If I say something and it works for the golfer, that golfer may begin to rely on me and less on him or herself. I am creating a dependency when it is the opposite of what I wish to do. I want you to be able to tell me that "I'm good now, James – I know myself, I like myself and I accept myself". You continue on your road to your destiny. I am simply here at the side of the road and you've popped in to say "can we figure something out together?" and when we do, we go our own way.'

'I feel like you are pushing me away. We've only just begun to work together and you're telling me that I'll be off on my own again.'

'You feel like I am abandoning you, Chris?'

'Yeah, the moment I find security in something it's being taken away from me...'

'Perhaps I have emphasised too early that we ought to rely upon ourselves more – I'm sorry. My intention is to highlight your strengths, your coping skills, and when it's appropriate to end our work together, I'm sure we will both agree about what is best. What we share together, and what we have shared together, is a confidence you might begin to share with others, and we can talk about that at another time...'

Chris chuckled and said, 'I think you are the first person I've met who does not want me to keep coming back. I work in a competitive business and I know that's not a good model! But then again, I suppose it goes to show that you have my best interests at heart. I guess I've realised that I wanted more out of this working relationship than is necessary. That's about boundaries, isn't it? I watched that on *In Treatment,* with the Irish shrink – Gabriel Byrne – have you seen it?'

'Yes I have,' said James.

'He's good – really good. He sees past the obvious. And even though he has his own troubles, he's got his clients' best interests at heart. Now....time to get back in the groove.'

Unfortunately, Chris' drive was blocked right and landed in some bushes in the rough. He quickly went through his routine again and played a provisional down the left-hand side of the fairway. Chris couldn't find his original ball and, so, had to play his provisional. He hit his fourth shot into a greenside bunker; and as Chris and James walked up towards the green, Chris asked James: 'How should I be feeling now?'

'I wonder how you are feeling now.'

'Good response! I'm a mix of emotions. I've hit good shots but the outcomes were not good – three off the tee and a greenside bunker – so I'm disappointed but not disturbed.'

'You're disappointed but what has happened is not bothering you too much – is that what you mean?'

65

'Yes, that's it. It's strange because I have a feeling inside me that I'm going to get up and down from here and that's OK. I'm rolling with it and that's kinda cool.'

Chris did get up and down from the greenside bunker. He had to hole an eight-foot putt too. When James placed the flag in the hole, he asked Chris to look back up the fairway and to tell him about what just happened on that hole.

'OK – I got this. I prepared well for my tee shot and really got through it. I did push it out to the right and lost my ball and I can accept that outcome. I don't enjoy it but I can accept it. I really enjoyed the flight of the ball from my 3-wood off the fairway. And when the ball landed in the bunker I felt OK. The ball landed in there and, strangely, I was excited to play the bunker shot. I played it well and walked off with a six.'

Then Chris paused for a moment and shook his head slowly, saying, 'You know, James, I'm lying about how I feel about the tee shot. I'm still really annoyed with myself....getting to the acceptance part is...well, a bit much for me right now.'

James smiled. 'If you're still back on the tee, we can wait a while until you're ready to move to the next tee?'

'Yeah, I like that. OK – come on, brain, you got another tee shot to play!'

Chris and James walked to the 13th tee. They looked over the sea, to the town, and to the beautiful image of St Andrews against the blue sky. Chris said, 'You know, whenever I walk along the beach there, I'm reminded, in my mind, of the Vangelis' music.'

'You mean, for the Chariots of Fire scene?'

'Yeah, that's the one – I love that film. It's a film about good things – important things,'

They chatted about the film and about Harold Abrahams and Eric Liddell and the 1924 Paris Olympics. They chatted about the good things – the important things.

Hole 13:
Hale Bopp (188-yard par 3)

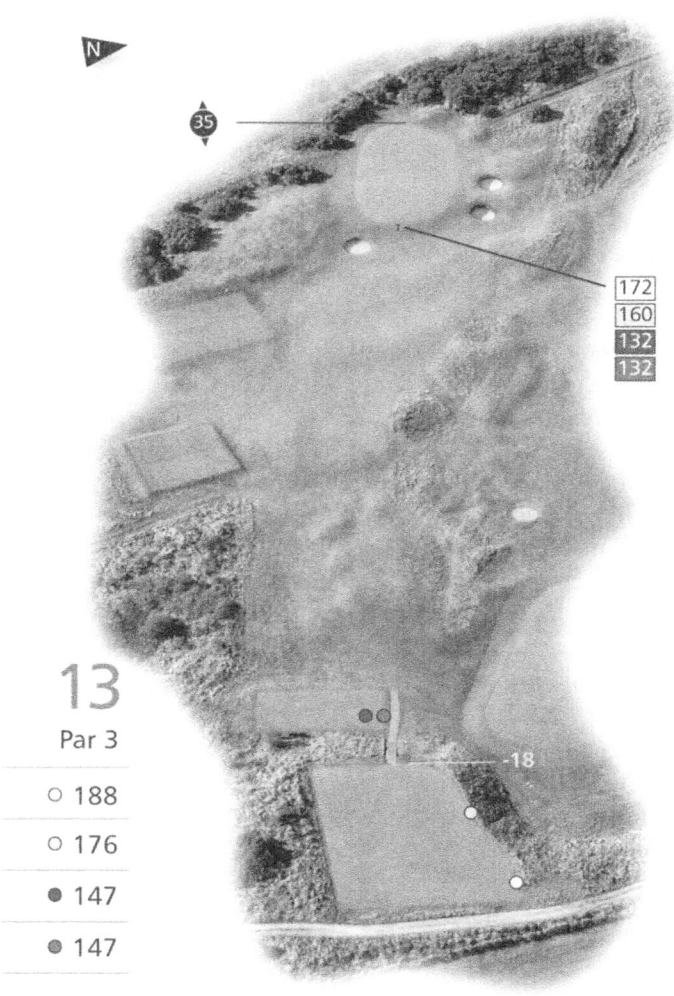

13
Par 3

○ 188
○ 176
● 147
● 147

As Chris turned back to his bag to select his club for the tee shot, he finished whistling Vangelis' famous theme tune and started to cajole himself. 'OK. Let's get ready for action. 188 yards…5-iron…nice and easy. You've got this, Chris.' Chris was a little more agitated and hesitant over the ball than he had been a few holes back and took an extra glance at the target, and one more waggle of the club, before starting his swing. The shot itself was perhaps steered a little, rather than struck confidently, but it found the front edge of the green, leaving a long putt for birdie.

After a deep exhalation, Chris spoke. 'Well, that felt like hard work, James. I have to say that I am really happy with that result. What's more important, I am really happy with how I managed myself to make that shot.'

'Tell me more about what you mean by that, Chris?' asked James.

'Well, like I said as we stood on the tee, I couldn't just let go of the bloody drive on the previous hole and I was battling away with myself. I was just trying to drown out all that negative crap and focus on this shot. I was trying to remember how I had been feeling a couple of holes back when every shot seemed so easy, but I couldn't quite get it. Still, I took my time and got a bit looser and a bit calmer, and then went for it. I just know that usually I would have played the shot while tight and upset with myself, and made a mess of it – giving me more good reason to beat myself up for not being able to hit the shot or deal with the pressure. Maybe you're right, James. Maybe I am starting to "get it". Maybe I can already apply some strategies to deal with the kinds of things that usually wreck my card … and my day.'

'Excellent work, Chris. That is exactly what I meant about you getting to know yourself and being able to help yourself. So what learning point will you take from that shot which you can apply again?'

'Well, apart from taking some pride in dealing with my negative chatter, I guess it is about taking time to sort out my thoughts before I start my swing.'

'That is nice, Chris. I like the fact that you took something quite "practical" – getting your pre-shot routine to work for your game, not against it; and something a little more personal –recognising when you should give yourself a pat on the back. Good work.'

'Yeah, it's funny, but while that shot was not as much fun as some of my recent ones where I was right in the zone, I enjoyed it in its own way. Well, maybe "enjoy" is a bit strong, but I am proud of it, at least. I have always found that it is easy to play great golf when things are going well for me, but when the wheels come off they come off big style. That last shot was a lesson to myself that I have some control even when things are tough.

Hold on a minute... I think I have had a bit of an epiphany, James. I just thought about Bob Rotella's book that "golf is not a game of perfect". I think I finally get what he means by that. For me, that is all about how I control myself when things are a bit difficult. It would be nice to play my A-game all the time but what I really need to make sure is that when it is not there, I at least have a B-game and not just spiral down to my Z-game! Hey, I hope you don't mind me quoting from one of your "competitors", James?' Chris finished with a smile.

'I'll forgive you this time, Chris... but only because I like you,' James responded lightheartedly. 'That is actually a great insight you have had there and it is nice to see you bring stuff together from your previous experiences and reading. We need to have an open mind to allow insights to emerge, and I am impressed with how you have done that during our walk today. It's important to keep yourself open to these insights that might come as you play or practice, as you never know when another piece of the puzzle may fall into place. Your subconscious may have worked out steps to help you play better golf before your conscious mind has even considered it. Does that make sense, Chris?'

'I think so, James. It's like they were there waiting just behind a door or something. Maybe it takes something to open up the door. I guess that is what you are trying to do today. Give me the right keys, or just some oil for the rusty hinges, eh?'

'That is an interesting way to look at our relationship. I think it is more like I helped you look for the keys or for the oil you already knew you had but had misplaced. After all, it was you who decided to take a bit longer over the last shot and calm down – that was your own coping strategy, Chris – not something I "gave" to you.'

'James ... you are a hard man to compliment, but I can see why it is important for me to realise that I can make a difference to my own game and that I should take pride in that. Anyway, I guess it's time I switch on again and take pride in sinking this putt.'

The putt didn't go in … but another tap in for par left Chris at level par after 13.

Hole 14:
Willie Whitelaw (438-yard par 4)

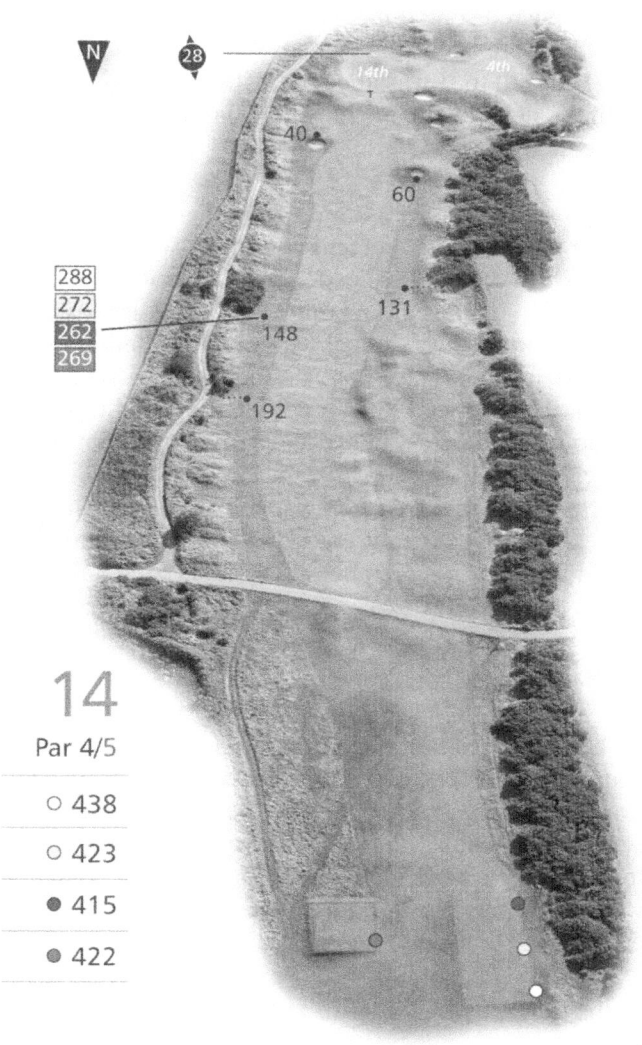

14
Par 4/5

○ 438
○ 423
● 415
● 422

Chris pulled his drive on the 14th into the rough, but it seemed like it was in a reasonable position, from the vantage point on the tee. The drive looked, at least to James, like a protective swing of the club and a response to his push on the last – a result he had come to know quite well in his own game, if truth be told. The fine line between controlling what we ought to do, and letting go, seemed as much a challenge for the psychologist, as it was for any golfer. On the face of it, James and Chris were using words to describe their thoughts, feelings and actions on the golf course; yet, it appeared something was missing in these transactions. The deep feelings that were occurring on and off the golf course for Chris were simply reduced to 'I was annoyed with that shot' or 'I couldn't cope with the nerves on that chip shot'. James began to explore the dilemma before them.

'Chris, I am going to switch roles for a moment to that of a teacher to allow me to uncover an important element within the work that I do and the psychological growth that you are experiencing in our work. One of the challenges we face in understanding ourselves is the upheaval in helping others to understand how we feel, without discounting or dismissing the importance of what we are sharing. It is my role to listen carefully, and in detail, to the story that you are telling, and to reflect that story back to you so that I am clear in my understanding about what you have shared. I depend on the words that you use to gain that understanding; yet, those words are often inadequate to explain how we feel. I can see the expressions on your face, how you hold yourself, and how you appear to me. Do you remember a few holes back I asked you about your "seven-year-old self"?'

'Yeah, I remember.'

'When your tee shot landed in the rough, I didn't actually know it. I was looking at you and how you appeared. I noticed your pursed lips, you chin sliding towards your chest, and your shoulders slump slightly. You appeared like what I would imagine is a seven-year-old who was told off when he couldn't figure out some math questions in school. What I am saying is that we show others how we feel in many of the ways we carry ourselves.'

'Are you saying that you can see how I'm feeling, without me having to explain it to you?'

'Yes, I suppose I am. It is not always accurate and I am often mistaken, though I see when there is a mismatch between what I hear and what I see.'

'Do you mean that my words sound hollow next to how I seem in my body?'

'Yes, Chris, you made your point perfectly. We can easily say things to other people that we truly do not feel, but it is our way of defending ourselves, given that sport is mostly played on a stage where we are judged and evaluated – a public stage.'

'I think I know what you mean. That I should be honest and not lie about what's going on inside, but I can't imagine that works well in golf, or any sport, because we are competing and we are giving an advantage to our opponent.'

'It's more of a matter for our work together and how you speak to yourself, rather than what happens in competition. But you do make an excellent point – competitive sport asks us to manage our impressions towards others – but that's worth discussing at another time. My interest now is about relating to our feelings, rather than denying them because they have meaning. We can find it easy to deny feelings because early in our lives our emotions got us into trouble. Do you remember what your parents said to you when you were younger and were frightened about something like the dark?'

'Yeah, they told me, "Don't be silly, there's nothing to be frightened about".'

'What about when you were angry?'

'Ah, that's a good one, because I would get into trouble and punished for fighting with my brother.'

'That's a common one for most people. When we were anxious we were told to "toughen up", and when we were jealous we were told we were "wicked"; yes, our emotions got us into trouble and the one way we could deal better with them was to deny those emotions. But, in the clear light of day, it does not seem to make sense to bury these feelings in a box like radioactive waste deep underground. Our emotions are helpful to us and they have served us well over thousands of years to help us survive. We need to understand our emotions and how they can help us, as well as those emotions that lead us in unhealthy ways.'

'It makes sense now that you have explained it that way. In fact, it makes a fine point.'

At this point, Chris had reached where his ball had landed. Although it was in the rough, he had a reasonable lie a few feet from the car path, but his best option under these circumstances was to advance the ball up the fairway. Chris steadied himself with some practice swings in the nearby rough to gauge the challenge before him. Once contented, he set up beside his ball and, with a studious expression upon his face, struck firmly down on the back of the ball, exploding it from the rough. The ball came to rest six feet from a fairway bunker lying 60 yards from the pin.

Chris paced steadily towards James and said solemnly, 'I get it.'

Somewhat perturbed, James enquired, 'What do you get, Chris?'

'I get the freedom you mentioned earlier to me – I really get it. But it's not just one thing, it's a collection of jigsaw pieces and if I do not fit the pieces together before I play a shot, then the outcome is an inevitable consequence. You see, I was turning over in my mind what you had said about emotions and how we learn that they get us into trouble. I realise now how much I was fighting them, and in my foolishness I thought I was the prizefighter unbeaten after another title fight, but I wasn't – I was nowhere near. I learned feelings were bad, especially guilt and shame. And even though I thought I was controlling them, they were actually controlling me. How does that sound to you, James?'

With the briefest hint of a smile, James replied, 'It sounds to me as though you recognise the price you have been paying to be perfect, the price you are paying to avoid failure at all costs in the eyes of other people. It sounds as though you have been dragging yourself before the harshest judge of all – you. You condemned yourself without a fair hearing.'

After a moment, James enquired, 'May I ask you where this realisation came from?'

'Well, that's the strangest thing; when I was taking my practice swings in the rough before I addressed my ball, clumps of grass came up on the clubface each time. As you know, the grass in the rough is not like the grass on the fairway but I don't mind the grass being that way; in fact, the rough adds to the rugged beauty of the golf course – they work well together. Whoever I am, good stuff and bad stuff, I'm OK, and I'm OK with being OK. Sometimes, I'm the fairway and, sometimes, I'm the rough but I wouldn't like to be all fairways, you see?'

'Yes, a lovely metaphor.'

'I played that shot well because I accepted that it was in the rough – I hit it in there – so I was responsible, and I went to find it, and I hit it back out. Simple – I didn't need to beat myself up. Since we left the tee box, I didn't get a chance to think about the outcome or, more accurately, dwell upon it and judge myself harshly – why should I judge myself harshly?'

'You recognise the difference now between doing something and doing something with evaluation?'

'Yes, I guess that's it. I know I probably can't do it all the time but I can certainly reduce the critical judge in me and see things in the round (pardon the pun!).'

Chris hit a fine shot into the green but missed the putt for par.

'I know this is not going to sound good but it is how I feel, James – I feel contented about what happened on that hole. I didn't make birdie, I didn't even make par. I dropped a shot. I'm OK with it.'

'What do you feel OK about, Chris?'

'Ah, good question. I feel like I can make mistakes, if that's even the right word, and accept it. I feel OK about not being perfect. I feel OK about being normal. And, you know, it gives me a sense of freedom or confidence; I'm not sure which one is correct but I know I'm looking forward to the next hole and my mind is coming with me – it's not back in the rough.'

Hole 15:
Steel's Gem (356-yard par 4)

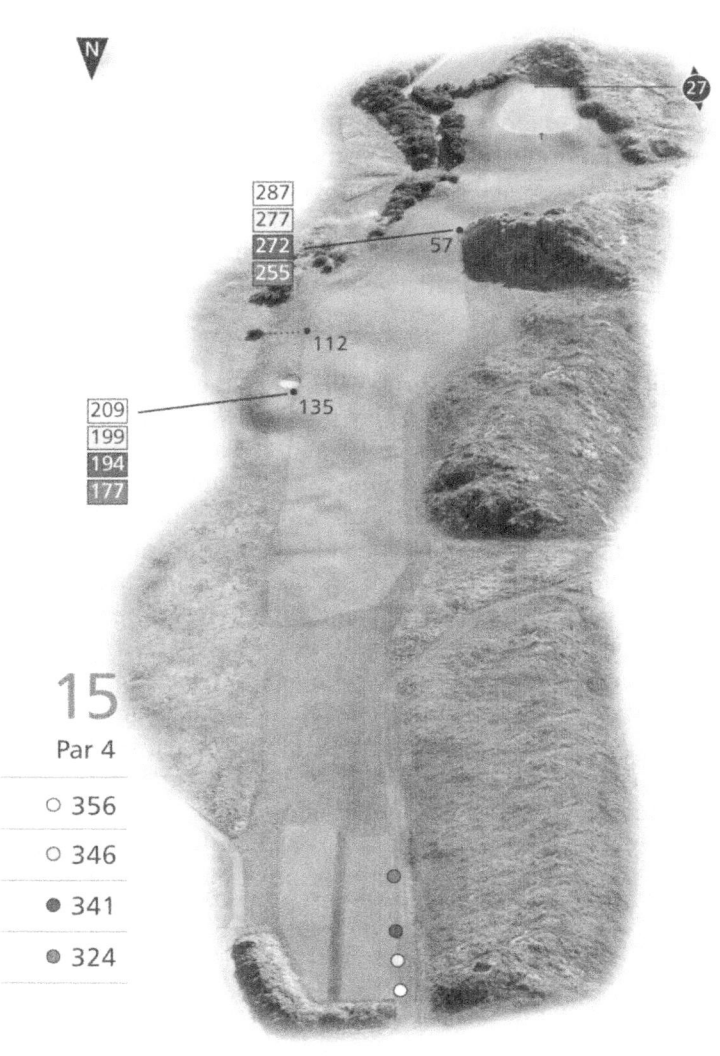

'Well, James, we haven't got long left. "Steel's Gem" always seems like the beginning of the end of the round to me. I'm going to try to enjoy every shot from now on and see if I can finish with a flourish. First up, a nice 3-wood draw up past that fairway bunker would be just the ticket.'

Unfortunately, the shot didn't draw, so Chris had left himself in the semi-rough off the right- hand side of the fairway and with a blind shot left into the raised green over a sand dune.

'Now, that is a bad place to miss on this hole, James, so I am unhappy with that. But…, (deep breath) you know, I took the right line off the tee and didn't quit on it or anything, so I can't be too upset with anything but my execution. I might not make perfect golf shots over the next four holes, but I damn sure will try to keep my thought processes on the right line. I've gone too far in this round to take a step backwards now in the way I talk to myself. In fact, as the next shot will be blind, I guess I can look at that as sort of a cool challenge and a chance to have fun with the course.'

James was interested to watch Chris stride down the fairway as if he couldn't wait to get to the ball and play his shot. While he had walked this way during his hot spell a few holes ago, it was not something he had been doing following shots when he was in trouble. Instead, he often seemed to be delaying getting to the ball – trying to put off the moment for as long as he could. The confident and purposeful walk was clearly a physical manifestation of Chris' more productive way of thinking – both in terms of how he evaluated his previous tee shot and prepared for his upcoming approach shot. James enjoyed watching the way that Chris was learning to manage himself and was confident that Chris would continue to make further steps forward with his mental game. He couldn't help but chuckle to himself to see Chris run out from behind the mound on the right-hand side of the fairway to check the flag location on the green and run back to his ball in the semi-rough – a bit like a kid might. He seemed to be enjoying the challenge of the shot rather than thinking what it might mean to his card - One of the key things he was working hard on during the round. His words and his actions seemed to be absolutely in synch.

Chris made a great swing and sent the ball high on a great line towards the flag on the left-hand side of the green. Unfortunately, he had mis-clubbed and came up a bit short, which meant that his ball hit the bank at the front of the green and ran down the hollow to the left of the green –

leaving a tricky little chip. James waited to hear what Chris would say about the shot.

'Where did that go, James? I thought I had hit a cracker there. I was expecting to see that close. Don't tell me I was short?'

'Afraid so, Chris – it was a great line but just caught the front bank and bounced left.'

'Arghh! You are joking!?… (shaking his head) That is really tough to take… (deep breath)… OK (deep breath)… Right, Chrissy boy. Well, it was a good strike, so let's see what you can do with this chip.'

Unfortunately, Chris' ball had ended up in a tough lie in the rough and he was only able to hack out to about fifteen feet, from where he lipped out for par. After tapping in for his bogey, he picked up his ball and smiled wryly over at James. 'Well, that would have been an "interesting" hole to be inside my head, James.'

James remained quiet, allowing Chris some time to get his thoughts together as they walked to the 16th tee. Chris took his time and seemed to be struggling to find the words to explain his feelings to James.

'A bogey was not exactly what I was looking for when we talked on the last tee, with me at 1-over par, I can tell you. It's hard to put into words how I am feeling about that hole. I felt really confident on the tee and I was a bit surprised, to be honest, that my tee shot was offline. I guess it was the perfect test for me to do what I said I wanted to do on the tee – trying to stay positive and play each shot with confidence. While the hole wasn't pretty, you know what? – I did manage to do that. I really had to work hard to get myself in a good mindset for each of those shots and I am working hard right now to take the positives from that. I was able to make each shot an individual challenge – the blind approach shot, the hard chip, and the putt down the hill. I gave myself a chance to make a good swing on each one of those, and that is all I can do. Actually, thinking back, I did that bloody well, and each shot was actually quite fun. That is the message I am going to take forward on to this tee. Let's have some fun with one of the coolest drives on the course!'

Hole 16:
Freddie Tait (428-yard par 4)

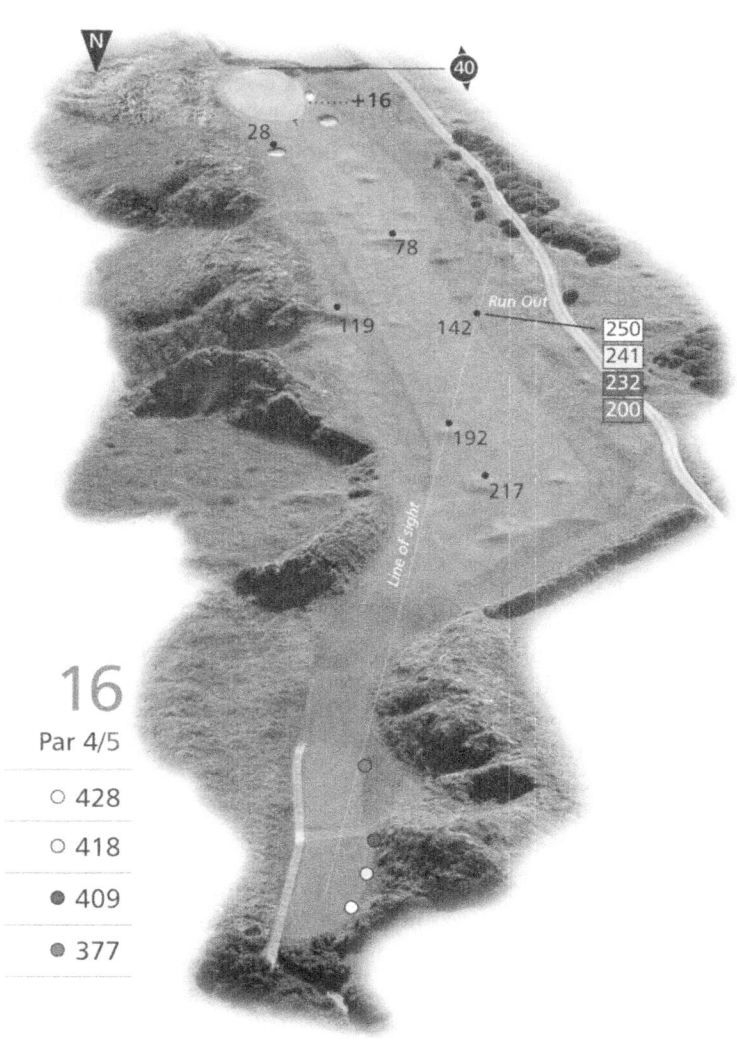

16

Par 4/5

○ 428

○ 418

● 409

● 377

The sixteenth is a 428-yard par 4 set in stunning undulating terrain. The narrow fairway screams for precision from the tee, yet it is this precision that warns golfers to "put the brakes on" and steer the ball to a fair position on the fairway. The right-hand side of the fairway rewards most golfers but the left-hand side is most penal.

James and Chris discussed this tee shot as they stood on the tee, waiting for the fairway to clear ahead. Chris explained to James how he was feeling.

'I'm in a reasonably good place looking back over the past fifteen holes but now I'm entering "no man's land". Chris had been reading about the First World War and this term "no man's land" – an area of land between the trenches of each enemy that neither side wished to seize for fear of attack – was how he felt about the last three holes. So often in the past he had teed off here with an unblemished scorecard, only to find himself writing numbers that made him feel angry with himself and despairingly about the game of golf.

'Do you mean you are protecting what you have when you play these last few holes?' James enquired, with a stress upon "protecting".

'Mmm – yeah, I suppose I am cosseted until I reach this point and I steer intently to not make mistakes.'

'Not make mistakes?'

'Yes, that's correct. I am trying not to make a big number on any of these holes – which, of course, rarely happens.'

'Your attempts to protect your score unwittingly open you to those "big numbers".'

Chris, recognising the obvious point now, had an answer to his plight. 'I see what you mean, James; I'm trying to do the impossible – play freely by not playing freely. To protect my score by thinking about my score and not attending to what I am supposed to do. It adds up.'

Chris stopped for a moment, replaced the 5-iron he was holding and selected his driver. 'If I'm going to learn, I guess I must risk something. If I'm going to overcome my fears, I must, at least, face them.'

Chris hit a lovely draw out to the right-hand side of the fairway, the ball moving slightly in the air – and as it fell to the ground it clipped the edge of the fairway, leaving him 138 yards to the pin.

Chris laughed out loud and proclaimed, 'Letting go is not easy – not easy at all – yet, it has all the answers. Can you explain that conundrum to me, James?'

'I wonder what it means to you, Chris. What does it feel like to "let go"?'

'You don't let me away with much, James, I'll give you that. All the answers are my answers – bloody clever! Well, I better answer my own question, then. I am a relatively cautious person, and the extremes of this behaviour you'll see in my work and golf, for some reason. When I do "let go", I feel light, happy, contented and it's a feeling all over my body. I can feel my face relax. But it doesn't end there because I feel in my head that I can do what I'm doing. It's a kind of a "OK, let's get amongst it". You know, the more I talk about it, the more I recognise my uptightness. I can show you the difference in my hands, well, my knuckles. I'm a "white-knuckle rider" on the roller coaster but I'm buzzing afterwards. Somehow, it's just not as scary as I think it is, but I've certainly got better at riding those. I have to feel like I don't care about the shot, when I know I do care about the shot. That probably sounds mad but I play best when I take my hands off the steering wheel, as it were.'

'Correct me if I've got this wrong, Chris; you have most fun when you consciously "let go" of those things that can work perfectly well on their own without your interference – like the roller coaster or the golf swing – when you trust that whoever is there to do the job can do it perfectly well without you?'

'Ah ha, that's it, I guess. It's learning to trust myself and I don't always.'

'That's something we can work on together away from the golf course. Yet, even today, you have shown great trust in yourself, which demonstrates your ability in that sense. We are often unaware of the trust we place in ourselves and others. A trust that repays on our investment and we can begin by working on ourselves. When we do not act, we cannot expect the good things to happen.'

Chris jumped in to say, 'So we are left with remorse and the remorseful day

"Ensanguining the skies

How heavily it dies

Into the west away;

Past touch and sight and sound

Not further to be found,

How hopeless under ground

Falls the remorseful day."

You look surprised James; you didn't expect that from me, now did you?'

A little flustered, James replied, 'I don't usually hear people recite poetry on the course.'

'Well, James, we had to learn it in school and, strangely, it stuck with me. I suppose you know which poem it is and by whom.'

James ventured, 'May, by A.E. Housman.'

'That's the one. How do you know it? No need to answer that, James; my stereotypical view of a psychologist will answer it: classical music, literature and poetry. Of course you'll know it. We had an English teacher from Shropshire who used to remind us about Housman and especially this poem, and how we should not let the day or life go by without doing what we say we are going to do.'

'You see, Chris, poets and writers and scientists, and all those who have gone before us have said it clearly – all of humanity has given us these answers – yet... yet, we are unwilling or unable to find gold in our world because we want someone to give it to us, rather than sweating and

84

toiling to have what it is we want. It is wishing without acting that leads us into the forlorn cul de sac. I see now, you, Chris, you have the answer.'

Chris walked to his ball. He assessed the challenge before him and, following his routine, he hit a 9-iron to the middle of the green that ran out to the hole. He holed his 10-foot putt – a left to right breaking putt that dropped in the "side door", and walked over to James.

'Thank you, James.'

'You're welcome, Chris.'

No more needed to be said. James and Chris were equals and now Chris knew it; to this point, he was reluctant to take responsibility for himself – to grow up psychologically, as it were. They were equals in every sense of the word. Chris said thanks to James – not for helping him, but for allowing him to see himself and begin on the road to helping himself. James recognised Chris' thanks. In that moment, Chris' words exactly matched his facial expression and body language. It was as if the emotion was there – gratitude, with healthy self-respect – in a mature and feeling person.

Hole 17:
Ladyhead (211-yard par 3)

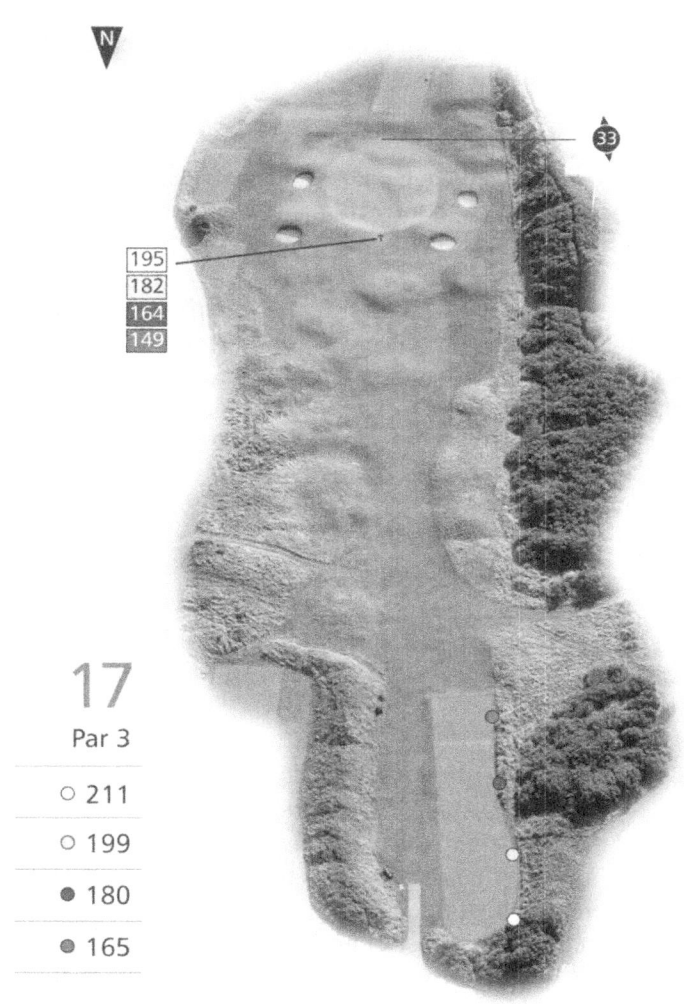

195
182
164
149

33

17

Par 3

○ 211

○ 199

● 180

● 165

'OK, two holes to go and then I can buy you a drink, James! Another birdie chance here, don't you think? Let's keep the good times rolling.' Chris stood on the back of the tee box, looking towards the flag and swinging his hybrid lazily back and forward. 'I guess the stock shot here is the fade, but I am seeing it as a nice high draw today.'

Chris looked relaxed and confident as he went through his pre-shot routine and had a small smile on his lips as he made his swing. The shot was powerfully struck and drew in from the right edge of the green, landing on the front edge and tracking towards the pin. Perhaps it was too well hit, or took a hard first bounce, but it carried to eighteen feet past and left of the hole.

'Great strike, Chris. I'd love to have taken a video of that swing to show you how content you looked, and how fluid and powerful your swing was. You looked like you were having the time of your life.'

'I honestly don't know where I would rather be when I feel like that. It is like magic or something. I saw the shape of the shot and hit it exactly as I saw it – drawing off the right-hand bunker. Magic… The company obviously helps too (nudging James with his elbow as they walked towards the green). And just have a look round James … (the sun was getting low in the steely sky, further dramatising the undulating links landscape) … how could I not feel great being here, playing this course? We are lucky buggers, you and I, James. I am glad you are here enjoying this view with me.'

'Me too, Chris. It's been a great journey so far and I'm looking forward to seeing how it pans out. Not just today, but as we travel down the line.'

The two men walked together down towards the green, comfortable in their silence, looking out over St Andrews Bay and enjoying the view.

As Chris dropped his bag behind the green near the 18th tee he turned again to James. 'It's funny, James, but I was thinking back to that throw-away sentence on the tee about the draw versus the fade. I swear that a thought like that could sometimes start me having a bloody debate with myself about what I should do. I would often carry that debate into my swing – and if I messed things up I would then beat myself up, while considering the consequences afterwards. Instead of beating myself up, here I am having the time of my life. All it took was for me to trust myself and enjoy the whole process of what playing golf means. See the shot I want to play, play that shot, and accept the consequences, repeat. It's really that simple for me.'

'That's a lovely insight, Chris. I might have to steal that one too. You are getting very good at this psychology stuff, you know.'

'I must have had a good teacher, I suppose.'

Joking aside, I am really proud of myself, James. I know I am capable of playing nice golf, and I know it feels easy then. But I have played some poor shots today, or had bad luck, and I've still been able to get back into a good mindset by just trusting myself and hitting the shot I see, on these last few holes. That is a new thing for me and it feels great; just feeling the trust and accepting what happens. Let's hole this and get onto the last.'

Chris lined up his putt and again hit the shot with a smile on his face. The putt looked dead centre all the way and Chris had his putter raised in celebration when it was a foot out. A sharp break as the ball slowed down caused it to horseshoe out on the high side. Chris dropped his putter and collapsed melodramatically onto his back. James walked over and, offering his hand, helped Chris up to his feet, while they both grinned like lunatics.

Hole 18:
Honeyman's Howe (351-yard par 4)

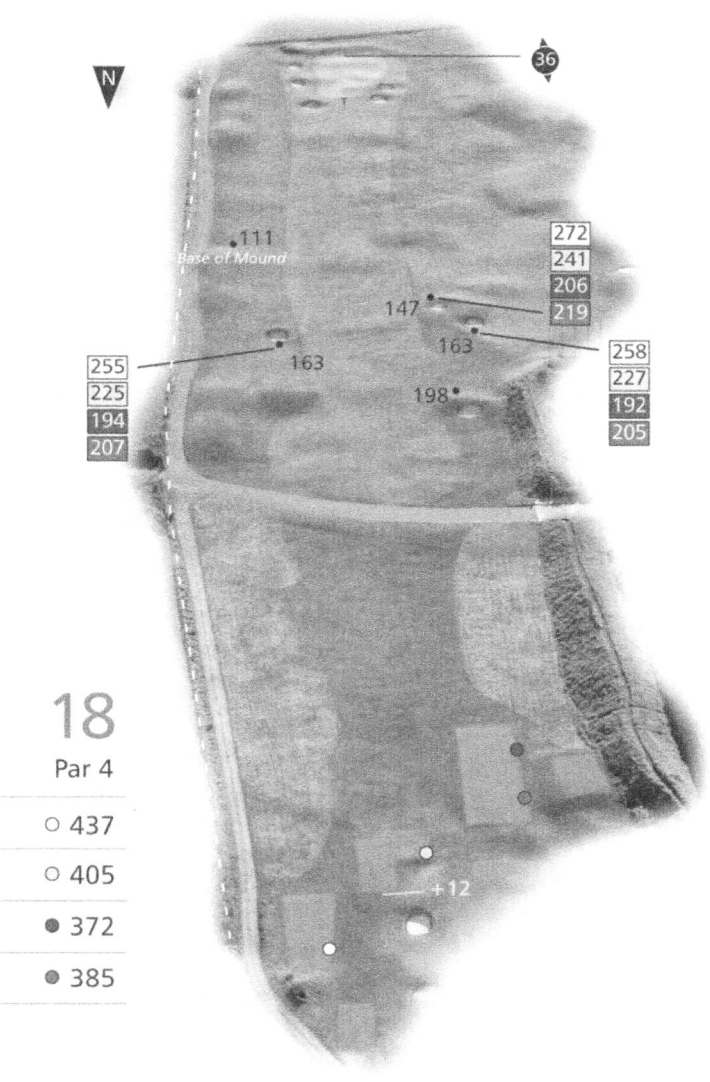

'This is the final hole, Chris; what do you want to do here?'

'I'm not sure I want to *do* anything, James; I want to enjoy the flight of the ball and the feeling of ease within my body and mind, but I'm not sure I want to do anything.'

'You seem to be suggesting that you have no absolute goal in mind here; is that right?'

'I guess it is, yeah. Is that OK?'

'You do not need my permission, Chris – you can take responsibility for your own actions.'

Inspired by this statement, Chris exclaimed, 'Indeed I can! And I am taking responsibility for my actions!'

Noticing the ludicrous statement he had just made – asking for permission when permission was not James' to give – made Chris laugh heartily.

'You know, James, I'm learning up to the last minute. I'm starting to really understand your position and mine in this relationship. I see us now as equals but at the start of this round I was willing, hoping and expecting you to advise and guide me towards better golf. I see that I was reluctant to accept responsibility for my actions. I wanted you to give me the answers.'

'And did I give you those answers, Chris?'

'No, not exactly; but you did help me to see myself better. And I can understand why you didn't give me the answers. If you gave me the answers, I would be forever chasing you for more answers, rarely – if ever – relying on myself. I would be dependent on you – like a child – not independent, now that I'm an adult.

But this relationship does not square with my relationship with my boss, my golf coach, my physiotherapist, my dentist, and so forth. Why is my position in these relationships as the underling?'

'Is that where you placed yourself, Chris, as the underling?'

Hearing this question, Chris again had to take stock and recall quickly his thoughts, feelings and behaviours in the company of these people.

'I suppose,' he ventured, 'I assumed this role in collusion with these situations. What I mean is that I saw myself as less than these people and, therefore, beneath them or subservient to them. And come to think of it, what is it but nonsense. I know that none of them can play the guitar and so, in my company, with this view point, they would be below me?'

'If you place your standing as a human being on achievement only,' James stated.

'Yes, I see what you mean. And I know that can't be right because I'm not just a guitar player. I'm a father, a husband, a brother, a son, an uncle, a golfer and many other fine things. And in the final analysis, I get to choose. I get to choose what I think and how I wish to feel. That really is true freedom. I guess that is what Victor Frankl was saying in his book about 'Man's Search for Meaning' – even in a hopeless place like a concentration camp, hope filled the minds of those who wanted to survive. They had a reason to live.'

'That's an insightful point and carries with it excellent counsel for our lives.'

'And yet, James, the game of golf goes on.'

Chris prepared for his tee shot. He looked content, and with a wry smile on his face, he settled over the ball. Two glances down the fairway and then, finally, back to the ball, and began his backswing. Although it looked as if it were such a slow swing from start to finish that it would not advance the ball beyond the red tees, Chris' swing unleashed the ball down the right-hand side of the fairway, hanging forever in the air before landing a few feet from the first cut of grass. If less was more, then Chris' swing proved it universally.

As he wrestled his tee from the ground, Chris said, 'James, that was Chris swinging his driver when he didn't need to do anything. This might sound strange, but I had a sort of flashback to when I was a kid practicing on the range while I prepared for that shot. I just saw myself in total freedom, hitting balls simply because I could – for the sheer, unencumbered expression of who I was and what I had learned to do.'

'Do you feel the two parts – you now, and you as a kid – had something in common?'

'Yeah, I do. I know what the commonality is now because I could see it clearly. My golf now is to prove to others how good I was when I was a teenager – a kind of yearning for my youth and my confidence in myself. And my golf as a teenager, well in the latter stages, was to prove to others how good I could be as an adult. And this is hard for me to say, but I wish I knew then what I know now. I'm left with the awful feeling of "what if", a regret of what I might have achieved. You see, at fourteen and fifteen I was excited about the future and it made the "here and now" so easy; and I was brimming with confidence. But as I got to sixteen and seventeen I was constantly undermining myself – I was a good golfer in spite of myself – but I knew something had got to give. I was so demanding, so unrelenting and so full of expectation. I used to think that other people lost faith in me but now….'

'But now…?' James enquired.

'But now I know I lost faith in myself.'

'It sounds as though you could see yourself and your aspirations ahead of you but, rather than running towards them, you were in a rowing boat, looking at them but rowing away from them. And the harder you rowed, the further away from the dream you were taken.'

'Yes, I like that metaphor. I always had my eyes on the prize but I was heading in the wrong direction. And because I was looking in the right direction but heading the wrong way, I thought I was doing all the right things.'

'It can often seem that way, Chris. And we dare not stop, in case we give up on our dream. We dare not take our eyes off the prize.'

Chris and James had arrived at Chris' ball. Chris had just over one hundred yards to the pin and set about his routine for the shot. Chris made three practice swings, smooth to a finish, and then stepped in behind the ball. Like his drive earlier, the metronomic swing dispatched the ball to a stopping position three feet from the pin. Chris stroked in the three-foot putt and picked out his ball while James replaced the pin. Going through the usual courtesy, Chris and James remove their hats and shook hands, and they made their way to the clubhouse. As they approached the clubhouse, Chris said, 'James, I feel like I've been on a journey – an emotional journey – pleasant in places and unpleasant in others. I didn't want to rake (pardon the pun) over the sadness and loss of what might have been, but I have a clearer picture in my head. A sort of edited version of the story I used to tell myself, if that makes sense?'

'Does it make sense to you, Chris?'

'Yes, it does. I feel I can learn about myself a little better now and I hope I can continue to learn about myself. If it is OK with you, I'd like to spend more time learning about myself, not just as a golfer but as a person too. I know it would be good for me and my relationships.'

Michael, a friend of Chris', who had recommended James to him, emerged from the club house and, after saying hello, asked how long it took him to get round.

'About thirty years,' Chris replied.

'What?' enquired Michael incredulously.

Then Chris looked at James, and Michael's eyes were drawn to him too. He realised Chris' witty remark and laughed, 'I've had the treatment, I know what you mean.'

Epilogue – 19th Hole (in the clubhouse)

James and Chris sat down to a table in a corner of the clubhouse. From here, they could see the contrast of the Old against the New (the Old Course and the New Course) and James took his lead from the links that, to all golfers, is home.

'What do you see from here, Chris?'

'How do you mean – what do you see from here?'

'You know, when you look out the window – what do you see?'

'Well, from this window I can see the Old course and the New Course, not all of them, of course (pardon the pun), just part of them. I see golfers out on both courses.' Feeling a touch nostalgic, Chris added, 'Everybody wants to play the Old and it's fantastic; but you know, the New is great too.'

James leaned a little further on this construction. 'The old has its charm and the new has its modernity?'

'Yeah, that's right. The Old is comfortable, like an old armchair, and the New is like a recliner – comfortable, too, but just takes a little getting used to.'

'What you have described sounds quite a lot like the work that I do, Chris. I work with change, and change is difficult for most people for lots of reasons; but I argue that change is good for us. It challenges us and stretches us. It helps us to keep adapting and building our resources for the challenges ahead. We can stick with the old ways and accept the consequences of thinking, feeling and behaving in that way, or we can choose to change to a new way of thinking, feeling and behaving. The choice really is ours,.

'I feel you are getting at something here, James, but I'm not sure if I understand exactly what you mean.'

'My central thesis here is that the work I do depends a little on me but much more on you. A commitment to change for the better is a commitment that only you can make. The old ways of doing things feels

97

comfortable and reassuring but we are left with the same dilemmas, whereas the new ways of doing things offers us a solution to the old problems. But the courage to change depends on you.'

'I see what you mean. Would you be able to tell me about someone that was like me and made the changes that were necessary? You see, I read Trevor Parr's book; and he wrote that chapter about how you helped him to like the golfer he was. He also wrote that Albert Ross had a similar challenge to overcome before he won the Open at Carnoustie.'

'Both stories were well publicised within the media and I guess you know them well by now. I have a code of confidentiality that prevents me from speaking about these particular cases but I can explain the psychology behind them without referring to any particular client.'

'I understand.'

'I can tell you about a client called Jim, who had been to see three sport psychologists before he came to see me.'

'Three sport psychologists? That doesn't sound good.'

'Yes, but that's also part of the story. Jim had played on tour for ten years and been in contention to win big tournaments on several occasions, but never succeeded. When he came to see me at my office I was caught off guard. He had flown in to do a photo shoot at the Old Course and came down to my office at the links unexpectedly. I did get a warning ten minutes before his arrival, from his agent, that he would be coming to see me. When he came through the door he was holding a copy of my book and threw it on the couch as he made himself comfortable. By the way, his agent didn't ask if I was busy or whether I had clients coming in; he just assumed that Jim would be the most important person in my timeline.

'Were you free at that time?' Chris enquired.

'As it happens, I was free for that hour. Jim's phone rang as he was making himself comfortable, so he took the call, which lasted about two minutes. And here's the conversation that ensued between us:

'I can't get a moment's peace – I can't see why they can't make a decision on their own – they can't change.'

Then his phone rang again and he answered it again, for another two minutes, before hanging up.

'Why they can't decide between the colours of the shirts is beyond me – my clothing business you see – our new line will be released soon.'

'What brings you to see me, Jim?'

'Did Trent not say when he called you?'

'No, he just said you'd be with me in ten minutes.'

'OK. Well, I was reading your book on the plane over here and I realised that I don't really like what those other sport psychologists were saying. I think they were wrong but I can see you'd be the right guy for me.'

'I wonder how you made that conclusion?'

'It's the way you say things – you can put it the way I like to hear it.'

'How do you like to hear it?'

'You know – stuff like "concentrated practice is the oil that keeps your game improving" and "the only change golfers accept is what they receive from the cashier". '

'What about those things that might be difficult to hear – how would you deal with those?'

'What do you mean?'

'Well, in the work that we might do together, we would meet challenges that are painful to explore and accept. You might, in the course of our work together, be confronted with the challenge to explore painful memories and "grow up" emotionally and psychologically.'

'That wouldn't be what I'm looking for at all. I've no problems on that score. It's more to do with my anger on the golf course. I just need ways to manage it.'

'Would you be willing to explore the origins of the anger you are feeling on the golf course?'

'Did you not hear me earlier; I've no problems on that score. I just need some techniques to manage my anger. I can add you to my payroll for the year, so we'll take care of you.'

'Jim, I'm not sure I can help you. It doesn't seem like you are ready to work with me yet.'

'Don't worry – I'll be ready to work with you. I've got to head off now so David (his agent) will be in touch with you to fly you out first class when I need you. You just let him know what you charge and he'll sort it. As I said, you'll be well looked after.'

'So what happened?'

'I spoke with his agent and explained the situation to him. I explained that a consultancy between us might not be possible at this moment. When Jim is ready to see me, I will be happy to see him.'

'But what about all the money and the perks – first class flights?' Chris asked incredulously.

'It's not a question of money or perks, Chris. It's a question of readiness for psychological change and all that it entails.'

'Well now! I understand the difference between "guru" and "chartered psychologist". It really does pay to see a qualified psychologist. The "guru" would have taken the cash. Have you seen that golfer since?'

'Yes, about twelve months later, I met him at a tournament in Florida. He said, "you saw in me what I was afraid to see in myself – a need for real change. I'm embarrassed by my arrogance when I went to see you in your office. I've been through a lot in the last six months, personally and professionally, and I know what you meant when you said that I was not ready to work with you yet. I'm ready now".'

'And did you work together?'

'Yes.'

'Can you tell me more?'

'I'm sorry; I can't talk about my consultancy.'

'I'm trying to guess who it might be, James, but I'll stop – it's unfair. But I do see what you mean. Change is difficult; even when we say we want to change, we might not be ready for real psychological change. And I know why, too – it's deeply emotional and it's a trade that's difficult to make. Yet, from what we did today, I see how wonderfully emancipating it can be.'

'So, James, would it be OK if we met next week as well. I would really like to lock in some of these insights and I think it would help if you were still there to support me.'

'Sure, Chris, I am free the same time next week.'

'Well, not quite the same time, James… I'll be here ten minutes earlier.'

Other Books from Bennion Kearny

The Successful Golfer: Practical Fixes for the Mental Game of Golf by Dr Paul McCarthy and Dr Marc Jones

Written by Dr Paul McCarthy (the first ever resident Sport Psychologist at St. Andrews Links) The Successful Golfer is designed to help address 50 of the most common faults that players experience and which hold them back. These include: hitting the self-destruct button when winning, nervousness on the first tee, losing focus off poor drives, and many more. Each fault is remedied with a clear practical fix. Readers will learn to develop effective practice plans, build a dependable pre-shot routine, cope with the pressures of competitive golf, and deal with distractions.

In the second part of the book, lessons from 30 fascinating research studies on golf are presented to help keep readers ahead of the field. They include research on putting, practice, choking, and overthinking. In the third and final part of the book, clear instructions are provided on developing a number of highly effective techniques that can be used across a wide variety of situations. These include: pre-shot routines, breathing exercises, goal setting, and how best to practice.

Golf Tough: Practice, Prepare, Perform and Progress
by Dan Abrahams

Dan Abrahams is Lead Psychologist for England Golf, as well as a former touring professional golfer, and PGA coach. In Golf Tough, Dan offers you a powerful blueprint for improvement and a detailed plan for consistent high performance no matter what your standard of play. If you want to significantly lower your handicap, compete with greater consistency, win tournaments or reach the next level on the course, Dan's simple yet powerful philosophies, tools and techniques will help you break through your current barriers and reach your golfing goals.

What Sport Psychology Can Teach Business: Ten Lessons for Peak Professional Performance
by Dr Martin Turner & Dr Jamie Barker

It goes without saying that business performance has many parallels with sporting performance. But did you realize that the scientific principles of sport psychology, used by elite athletes the world over, are being used by some of the most successful business professionals? Performance - in any context - is about utilizing and deploying every possible resource to fulfil your potential.

With this book you will develop the most important weapon you need to succeed in business: your mental approach to performance. This book reveals the secrets of the winning mind by exploring the strategies and techniques used by the most successful athletes and professionals on the planet.

Lightning Source UK Ltd.
Milton Keynes UK
UKOW06f2149090615

253215UK00015B/391/P